Linda Gerchick's
Practical Guide to Commercial Real Estate

Copyright © 2019 by Linda Gerchick

All rights reserved, including the right of reproduction in whole or in part, in any format.

First edition, 2019

DEDICATION

This book is dedicated to Tom Head, my partner and my rock, since the day I started down the road to investing in real estate.

CONTENTS

FORWARD
Why I Wrote This Book for Investors viii

BACKGROUND
About Linda Gerchick, CCIM x
What is a CCIM? xii

Chapter 1 — THE BASICS
How to Make the Market Work for You!™ 14
Purchasing Investment Property 16
Sound Advice for the Small Investor Planning to Build
    a Commercial Real Estate Portfolio 18
Top 10 Investment Considerations 19
Tools That are Used in Today's World to 'Find and Analyze the Deals' 23

Chapter 2 — TYPES OF INVESTMENTS
Single-Family as a Good Way to Start Your Portfolio 25
Multifamily Investments 26
What is a Triple Net (NNN)? 27
Fix-and-Flip or Value-Add Market 29

Chapter 3 — 1031 TAX-DEFERRED EXCHANGE

Why Exchange? 33
How It All Started: Starker vs. United States 33
The Basics of an Exchange 34
The Timelines and Identification Period 34
Identifying Properties 34
The Exchange Process 35

Chapter 4 — TYPES OF ENTITIES

Arizona LLC 36
Arizona LP 38

Chapter 5 — INSURANCE

Rehab Insurance 40
Buy-and-Hold Policies 40
Liability for LLC or LP 41
Extra Note on Insurance 41

Chapter 6 — TITLE AND ESCROW

Life of an Escrow 42
What is a Closing Protection Letter and What Does it
      Protect the Buyer/Seller From? 44
Critical Date Letter 45
Explanation of a Preliminary Title Report 45
Title Insurance 48
Hold Open Policies and Why are They Needed 50

Chapter 7 — PROPERTY MANAGEMENT

Property Management is Not for Everyone 52
What are the Duties of a Property Manager? 53
Transition into Property Management 55
Transaction Privilege Tax for Rentals 57
Capital Expenditure 58
Rent Rolls and Their Importance in Real Estate Investing 60
Landlord's Responsibility When it Comes to Federal Fair Housing 61
Routine Maintenance in Property Management 63
Why Do Background Checks on Tenants? 65
Evictions are Part of Real Estate Investing 66
Health and Safety Notices in Property Management 67

Chapter 8 — PROPERTY INSPECTIONS

Home Inspections (1-4 Units) 69
Commercial Inspections 70
Entering Every Unit 71
Sewer Cameras 72
Termite Inspections 73

Chapter 9 — DOCUMENTATION

What Kind of Items Do You Need for Your Due Diligence? 74
Do You Need to Install a Laundry Room? 75

Chapter 10 — FOREIGN NATIONALS

Canadians Investing in the USA 78
Other Nationals Investing in the USA 82

Chaper 11 — TAXES AND THE IMPLICATIONS
Tax Benefits of a Business in Real Estate 84
The Tax Cuts and Jobs Act of 2017 – Highlights 88

Chapter 12 — HOW DO YOU PAY FOR THE PROPERTY?
Single-Family to Fourplex Investment Financing 91
Multifamily and Commercial Investment Financing 92
Differences Between Bridge and Mezzanine Financing 97

Chapter 13 — FORMULAS
What is the Capitalization Rate? 99
What is the Loan-to-Value (LTV) Ratio? 100
Breaking Down Debt Service Coverage Ratio (DSCR) 100
Net Present Value (NPV) 101
Cash-on-Cash Return 102
What is the Internal Rate of Return? 102

Chapter 14 — HOW TO USE AND UNDERSTAND SPREADSHEETS
How to Use and Understand Spreadsheets 106
Investment Analysis — Single-Family 108
Investment Analysis —Fourplex 112
Investment Analysis — 10-Unit 116

INVESTING GLOSSARY 120

CONTACT INFORMATION 128

FOREWARD

Why I Wrote This Book for Investors

I love commercial real estate and facilitating great deals for my clients. I savor everything about the process: identifying a property, doing the due diligence, sourcing the project, negotiating with counterparts on the other side and finally bringing the best, most profitable agreement to the closing table that I can for all parties involved.

For the past 25 years, I have lived and breathed real estate for just about every minute of every day. Because to excel in this industry, you have to devote countless hours to learning the market nuances, understanding trend lines and what's going to happen before it happens, investing in continuing education and utilizing the latest in constantly-changing technology so you are always at the top of your game.

During that time, I have developed relationships with a vast number of developers, lenders, investors, agents, brokers, property managers, accountants, attorneys, escrow officers, title company representatives … you name it … and I been fortunate to tap into the incredible resources they offer.

Through networking, research and hands-on experience, I've amassed a wealth of knowledge of my own which I have been happy to share with others – from high-net-worth investors to mom-and-pop businesses and those just beginning their commercial investing journeys – through seminars, multi-day presentations and speaking engagements across the country and in Canada.

Usually, those teaching events have focused on one or just a few aspects involved in commercial real estate investing. But this is a vastly complex arena in which we work!

Have you ever gone to your local book store, or to Amazon, or just done a Google search looking for a book that brings it all together?

Amazingly, those publications are nowhere to be found. (Or at least they are extremely well hidden!) Which is one major reason I decided to write this book for investors like you: To create a resource with basic, unbiased and comprehensive, how-to information about investing in commercial real estate.

That dovetails with my strong desire to pay it forward and provide others with the knowledge that can help them succeed as I have in this fascinating industry.

As many of my clients and colleagues know, I have two young grandsons now to whom I am devoting much more of my time. That doesn't mean I won't still be involved in commercial real estate investing – it IS my passion, after all! – but what it does mean is that I will not be providing any more of the small group presentations and seminars that I have been known for in the past.

So, let this book be my way of giving back and ensuring you receive the full benefit of my knowledge on this subject.

I want every investor or would-be investor to succeed wildly in their commercial real estate endeavors. I hope what I have learned and am passing on to you now will help make that a reality.

What a legacy that would be!

BACKGROUND

About Linda Gerchick, CCIM

Linda has been in the real estate business for more than 25 years and has a well-rounded track record in advising buyers and sellers as a Commercial Broker and consultant. She has extensive experience in developing successful working relationships with clients, buying and selling, as well as in bringing together an entire team of professionals to help her clients with their commercial real estate investments.

After so many fulfilling years focused on serving her clients and growing Gerchick Real Estate, Linda has a new mission: Giving back, by sharing her vast knowledge of commercial real estate investing amassed by working with the largest developers, to mom-and-pop operations, to beginning investors.

While still being involved in this exciting industry niche and continuing to operate her highly successful boutique brokerage, Linda is taking a step back, so that she can devote more time to family (notably, her two precious grandsons) and to her own interests. But clients may be assured that she remains attuned to their needs and interests and will always provide her signature unmatched level of expertise and customer support.

Linda was born in Nebraska and raised in Phoenix, living in the Valley of the Sun most of her life. Early in her career Linda bred, raised and sold Arabian horses. Her ability to work well with both seasoned and first-time investors was instilled in her at an early age when she sold horses to a wide range of clients — from the Prince of Saudi Arabia to small rural families. She learned the art of negotiating from Dr. Armand Hammer and polished her skills in dealing with Arabian horse investments. This provided a perfect segue into real estate, where she drives a hard bargain for her clients on a daily basis.

In today's market it is important for a buyer's agent to possess knowledge and experience in bank foreclosures and short sales. Linda's extensive experience negotiating with banks and buyers through this process offers her clients peace of mind that their transactions will proceed to close of escrow as quickly and smoothly as possible.

Linda also has increasingly been assisting clients with the valuation, acquisition and stabilization of REO and distressed commercial real estate projects. She partners with a strategic advisory team that consists of CCIM members and other brokers and developers around the country to source and finance various commercial real estate opportunities with a focus in the multifamily arena.

She has sold over 2,500 fourplexes and a plethora of apartment buildings, office buildings and retail centers, among other properties. Linda was with RE/MAX Commercial Investment for seven years where she was ranked #2 and #4 in Commercial Closed Sales in the world, two consecutive years. She was recruited by Keller Williams Commercial in 2009 to head up the Northeast Valley office's commercial division.

In 2015, Linda fulfilled a longtime goal and established her own boutique brokerage and now is very proud to be the cornerstone of Gerchick Real Estate. Linda was also recognized as a "Deal Maker" by LoopNet Inc., which is the #1 commercial real estate service online, with more site traffic, more members and more geographic coverage than any other company.

Linda has been a part of the elite CCIM (Certified Commercial Investment Member) group since 2005. Linda has given seminars throughout Arizona, California and Canada, sharing her extensive knowledge. She provides free tools and information to investors through her website and has hosted many on visits to explore and invest in the Phoenix market.

Certified Commercial Investment Member (CCIM)

- Linda is an expert in the commercial and investment real estate market
- If you own, invest in or use commercial real estate, you need a CCIM
- Only 15,000 professionals are designated as CCIM worldwide

Recognition of Excellence

- CCIM curriculum reveals core knowledge of commercial investment practitioners
- Ability to deal with the diversity in the market/industry

Five Courses of Distinction

- Ethics
- Financial Analysis
- Market Analysis
- User Decision Analysis
- Investment Analysis for Commercial Investment Real Estate

Continuing Education in a Dynamic Business

- Resume of closed transaction and consultations, demonstrating depth of experience
- Comprehensive Examination to Earn CCIM designation
- Linda is proficient in theory and practice
- Continuing education after the CCIM designation is earned to master new subjects in the dynamic business of real estate

Most Coveted and Respected Designation in the Business

- Only 6 percent of all commercial real estate practitioners hold this elite designation
- Membership mirrors the changing nature of the industry
- CCIMs complete approximately 156,000 transactions annually, representing $400 billion
- There are 12 CCIM regions representing 1,000 cities
- The CCIM designation was established in 1969
- Courses leading to the designation are now offered throughout the world

What is a CCIM?

The Designation

CCIM stands for Certified Commercial Investment Member. The CCIM lapel pin denotes that the wearer has completed advanced course work in financial and market analysis and has demonstrated extensive experience in the commercial real estate industry. CCIM designees are recognized as leading experts in commercial investment real estate.

Investment Expertise

Above all, the CCIM designation represents proven expertise in financial, market and investment analysis, in addition to negotiation. Courses in these core competencies are taught by industry professionals, ensuring all material reflects the state of the industry.

With this real-world education, CCIM designees are able to help their clients:

- Minimize risk
- Enhance credibility
- Make informed decisions
- Close more deals

Who Earns the CCIM Designation?

Any commercial real estate professional is eligible to enroll in designation courses and ultimately apply to receive the distinction. Current designees include:

- Brokers
- Leasing professionals
- Investment counselors
- Asset managers
- Appraisers
- Corporate real estate executives
- Property managers
- Developers
- Institutional investors
- Commercial lenders
- Portfolio managers (loan servicing)
- Attorneys
- Bankers
- Other allied professionals

Chapter 1
THE BASICS

How to Make the Market Work For You™

Finding the right property for the investor is sometimes a very complicated assignment. It takes not only open communication between the investor and the real estate Broker, but also the ability to meet all of the needs of the investor's real estate portfolio and goals.

First and foremost, make sure that the real estate Broker LISTENS and has the correct kind of knowledge to work with the investor. Make sure that he or she has a clear understanding of short- and long-term investment goals. Be open and clear with this person. You can consider this person to be the backbone or quarterback of your real estate investment portfolio. Does he or she communicate quickly? How about answering the phone, text or emails?

Be really upfront about your financial resources. Really be clear about your risk tolerance. Are you a short-term investor or a long-term investor? This clearly can change the type of investment that is needed. What is your tax strategy?

A good investment real estate Broker will have a good team of referral partners in place. This could include a real estate attorney, CPA, property manager, title and escrow, and much more. If the Broker is well experienced, this process should be easy. DO NOT use an agent who is NEW! DO NOT use your best friend or neighbor!

Here is another strong recommendation: Do not use a Broker who does not OWN investment property himself or herself! Also, be sure that the Broker specializes in the type of asset class that you want to own.

Be sure that the Broker is well connected in the market. This should mean the Broker will "see" opportunities prior to the general public. It also means the Broker can send his or her own listings to experienced Brokers who have the client base that could shorten the listings' time on the market.

CHAPTER 1 — THE BASICS

It is also important to take into consideration that the property, if it is going to be leveraged, meets the lender's qualifications and that the investor meets the criteria of the lender. Evaluating the books and records, knowing the market and understanding the deal all need to happen before an offer is made.

It is important in an active market to get the asset nailed into contract. This may mean full or over-full price. It truly hurts investors to gain the reputation of low-balling their offers. While many of the real estate books and seminars will tell investors to offer 10 or 20 percent below what the property is listed for, this may not be the successful approach. Perhaps offering the full price and readjusting after inspections or appraisal is the way to go.

The Broker should make sure that the investor is using the best type of entity to make his or her purchase. A good Broker will make an effort to team up with some of the best CPAs and lawyers to help the investor make educated decisions regarding his or her entities.

Once all of these things have been handled, start the physical inspection with the property inspectors —make sure that whatever kinds of inspections are required by the investor and the lender are taken care of. This work should be done with the least amount of disturbance to the tenants. Sometimes it looks like many people are involved on the same day; that's on purpose. It is important to try to schedule everything at the same time while everyone is on the property site.

Referral Partners = The Best Support Team in Town

"Hire people who are better than you are, then leave them to get on with it. Look for people who will aim for the remarkable, who will not settle for the routine." — David Ogilvy

While the Broker may specialize in identifying income-generating properties and developing investment strategies, he or she should rely heavily on their team of industry leaders to assist with setting up the legal and financial entities and accounts. The support team should include: a real estate attorney who will provide counsel and prepare investment identities (such as an LLP, a Limited Liability Partnership), CPA (Certified Public Accountant) to assist with tax implications and banking specialists who can establish bank accounts to simplify the process of transferring funds. Investors should involve the property management in an early stage, as well as Escrow & Title and home warranty representatives.

"In this world, you get what you pay for." — Kurt Vonnegut, "Cat's Cradle"

There are appropriate fees associated with the attorney and the CPA. Other services are either commissions or standard industry fees assessed as part of the transaction. Home inspectors, surveyors and other service providers charge fees commensurate with the scope of the task.

Make sure that the Broker considers working with "the fairest" as a part of the assessment of working with "the best." While it is not possible to quote any actual costs, as each is related to the individual transaction, the fees are normal and consistent with the transaction. It is important to note that once a property is identified, the agent or escrow officer can provide some "working numbers."

Full Turnkey Solution

"Anything worth doing, is worth doing right." — Hunter S. Thompson

Engage a Broker who is so involved and passionate that their "real talent" comes from sensing industry changes and immediately acting. Clients can trust such a Broker when he or she calls with an opportunity to buy a property or to suggest that the investor sell a property.

In Summary

"A good reputation is more valuable than money." — Publilius Syrus

This sentiment is as meaningful today as it was in the 1st Century B.C. The Broker and his or her team are certainly in this business to make money for their investors and themselves, but never at the risk or detriment of their reputation or their clients. The Broker should be tough but fair and manage to represent his or her clients' needs while "playing fair" with colleagues.

While the Broker cannot claim to control THE market, he or she should be in complete control of THEIR market, which means watching, guiding, directing and caring for all those who work with and for him or her.

Purchasing Investment Property

Once you have decided to purchase real estate to meet your investment goals you should use your real estate Broker to identify and purchase your investment property. The first step is to form a relationship with an experienced real estate Broker. Never think that going to every real estate Broker who is well qualified in the market will get you a better deal; it WON'T!

Good Brokers and the best Brokers speak to each other often, and if someone is shopping Brokers, they usually go to the bottom of the list. Great investments are hard to find, and most Brokers will either send these deals to their proven clients or to the client who is

CHAPTER 1 — THE BASICS

working only with them. So, the best advice is to tell you to "pick your horse and ride it," so to speak. A qualified Broker can help you identify your investment goals and the right real estate vehicle to reach those goals.

This Broker will help you identify the property that meets your investment specifications by doing an in-depth cash flow analysis and keeping you informed of the latest market trends relevant to your purchase. The cash flow analysis will perform the dual role of 1) analyzing the true cost of acquisition and management of the property and 2) providing the buyer with realistic expectations for his or her investment's required contributions and subsequent profits.

The working relationship you form with your Broker will include making sure you are fully informed of all your due diligence throughout the acquisition process and negotiating the best possible deal among you, the buyer and the seller. Your agent will have fiduciary duty to you alone and will always protect your interests. This relationship goes beyond the purchase of your property and extends into the holding period of the investment property by keeping you informed of the current market conditions affecting your real estate investment.

Your Broker will provide recommendations for established and experienced property management companies that will be managing and protecting your property and will be a resource for you for facilitating good communication and problem-solving during the holding period of your investment. Your Broker will network you with complementary professionals, such as real estate CPAs, attorneys and 1031 Qualified Intermediaries as needed and will help you identify the best professionals for your individual needs.

Finally, your Broker will help you plan an exit strategy for the sale of your property. This plan will be based on your investment goals, current market conditions and the performance of the property. When it is time for the sale of your property, your Broker will help you maximize your purchasing power for your next investment and minimize your tax consequences by utilizing the tax deferment of the 1031 Exchange, if possible. The Broker should be able to guide you through the 1031 process, transitioning you seamlessly into the next level of your investment goals, making sure you perform within the guidelines established by the IRS.

This Broker should stand out in the real estate market in his or her complete package approach to investing in real estate. The Broker will assist you through every stage of the purchase and help you maximize your investment to its greatest profit potential. This Broker should have the experience and ability to address the needs and concerns of the first-time buyer as well as the in-depth market analysis required by the more seasoned real estate investor and to truly "Make the Market Work for You!" As you can see, the Broker that you choose is the most important piece of the investment portfolio.

Sound Advice for the Small Investor Planning to Build a Commercial Real Estate Portfolio

Individual stocks and bonds. Mutual funds. Precious metals. Options. Certificates of deposit and interest-bearing checking accounts.

Ask the "average" investor where he or she directs investment money, and more than likely the answer will include one or more of the vehicles listed above. But what other options are available to the investor who wants to truly diversify his or her portfolio?

Commercial investment real estate may be that option. For the individual willing to take on a little work and research, commercial properties offer a wide range of alternatives, from small multifamily apartment buildings to strip shopping centers to self-storage warehouses. And, with the high-tech sector slowing down from the highflying 1990s, many investors have learned the importance of diversification. The long-term outlook for investment properties is strong.

There's a tremendous range of commercial properties available for the small investor to consider. Each type of property presents its own potential for returns, management responsibilities and, of course, levels of risk. Higher levels of risk assumed in owning a particular property are usually rewarded with greater returns. However, even a low- to medium-risk property that is well-managed and properly financed can yield significant returns over the long term.

Investors making a first-time foray into investment real estate should keep the following in mind before purchasing a commercial property:

• Establish a Realistic Objective

Just as one would with stocks and bonds, an investor planning to purchase a commercial property should set objectives that are defined and attainable. Since returns on leased commercial properties aren't subject to the short-term roller-coaster ups and downs of Bay Street (Canada) or Wall Street, investors should not expect dramatic short-term returns during the ownership. Smart investors, however, determine an exit strategy for the disposition of a property at a prescribed time, preferably when the property has appreciated in value and market demand is strong. Identify what factors may trigger the sale (retirement, the purchase of a new home, relocation, etc.), and keep in mind the following: Real estate — governed in part by the economic principle of supply and demand — is not always a liquid asset.

• Add Sweat Equity

Add to the bottom line by investing personal time in the upkeep and management of the property. General remodeling tasks, minor interior and exterior maintenance, general accounting and other related chores often can be completed by the investor. This helps reduce overhead costs while letting the investor be more of a "hands-on" property owner.

• Avoid Highly Leveraged Deals

A highly leveraged financing package is one in which a small amount of cash is used to purchase a large or expensive property investment. These types of deals can prove extremely risky if capital improvements need to be made to a property and the investor has minimal reserves. Furthermore, a market fluctuation can outpace income. It is best to leave highly leveraged deals to experienced investors, which of course, you can all become.

Commercial real estate, like any long-term investment, presents great opportunity and inherent risk. A commercial specialist experienced in appraisal, brokerage, management, financing and other related areas can prove invaluable to first-time investors in helping to select an appropriate property, minimize risks and chart a long-term path to success. Select a real estate professional who has been educated in dealing with these and other issues that may surface during the anticipated length of time the property will be held. Also, find an experienced tax advisor who can help explain liabilities and strategies involving the Capital Cost Allowance.

There's plenty of capital available in the marketplace right now, and opportunities are available in the commercial sector for investors willing to take some risks. Like any speculative venture, investment real estate may not always perform up to short-term expectations. Over the long term, however, a well-managed and properly financed piece of commercial property unquestionably can prove to be a solid investment.

Top 10 Investment Considerations

1 — Owning Property in Personal Name

There are several different ways to take title when purchasing a property in the United States. Some may sound familiar (e.g., Joint Tenants), but as the buyer, an investor will need to understand how each different method can work for or against them. For example, if not purchased properly, Joint Tenants with Rights of Survivorship can have adverse estate tax effects on the survivor, whereas Community Property or Tenants in Common may prevent these adverse estate tax effects, regardless of the source of the funds used to purchase the property. With the proper advice, you can avoid costly mistakes and take advantage of the same opportunities.

Another consideration is liability exposure. If you are renting your property, you are exposing yourself to more risk than if you occupy the home yourself. When taking the title in your own name, you are personally responsible for any liability issues that arise. Although you can purchase insurance to protect yourself from some liability, your liability is unlimited and the insurance coverage may not be enough to cover the liability, whereas using a business entity may limit your liability.

Here is a thought that can be encountered in purchasing in your own name and thinking that the insurance will cover you: HAVE YOU EVER READ AN INSURANCE POLICY? Insurance policies tend to spend more time explaining what they do NOT cover than what they will. Read one sometime — even your automobile policy; it is really eye-opening!

2 — Owning Property Through a Foreign Company

This is one of the most common mistakes that people make when purchasing property in the U.S. While you may desire to keep all of your investments within one entity, the very act of owning U.S. real property within your company causes additional tax filing requirements and can cause adverse tax results, including potential double taxation. In the rare occasion that the benefits of owning property in a Canadian entity outweigh the cost, this is an exception to the general rule and should not be considered without the proper cross-border tax advice. Additionally, there could be jurisdictional disputes that would increase your legal fees.

Some states even consider an entity that is formed in another state to be a foreign entity. Often is it more prudent to go ahead and form the entity in the state in which the property is located. The reason (check with each state) is the filing and paperwork may be the same and you may be creating a situation in which you will need to file (for the property) an income tax statement for each state.

3 — U.S. Business Structures

How do you protect yourself against the liability associated with an income-producing property (e.g., rental property), yet not have the double tax or burdensome tax reports that are associated with a foreign entity? Deciding which business structures to use can be the difference in having positive or negative cash flow.

The optimum tax structure will depend on three sets of laws: the U.S. tax law, your home country's tax law (Canada), and the U.S.-Canada tax treaty. Without looking at the ramifications in each of these three separate taxing authorities, you run the risk of getting hit with a double tax, additional taxes, additional tax filing and the aggravation, time and money it takes to correct the corporate structure. Doing it right the first time is critical!

This is often called "getting papered up," and later in the book we will break down the different entities that can be used.

If you are buying multiple properties, there may be ways to structure the purchases in a more overall cost-effective manner.

4 — Income Tax

Once you own real property in the U.S., you may have a tax filing and liability in the U.S. attributable to this income. If the property that you own produces any revenue (e.g., rental income or capital gains on sale), you will be required to file tax returns. If the investor is a non-resident, the U.S. tax return needs to be filled by June 30th the year following the creation of the income.

Here is a catch for Canadian investors: The returns for Canada must be filed by April 30th in Canada. This means that the U.S. return must be filed prior to the Canadian, so really the Canadian investor must file the U.S. return prior to April 30th so that it can be included with the Canadian return.

For example, if you sold your U.S. property in 2018, the income tax return is due by June 30, 2019. However, as stated above, the investor will want to file early so the investor's Canadian accountant can file the Canadian return and take the appropriate tax credit.

5 — Estate Tax or Death Tax

The U.S. estate tax is computed on the Fair Market Value (FMV) of the assets at the time of death. Therefore, even if the property is worth less than what you bought it for, the investor bears tax liability. As a rule, non-residents of the U.S. are allowed to exempt $60,000 of their U.S. estate tax; US $120,000 for married couples. Under the U.S.-Canada Tax Treaty, Canadians are allowed a pro-rata amount of the U.S. resident exemption, which is currently US $5,000,000 (2011/2012). In many cases, the pro-rata amount is sufficient to exempt U.S. property from U.S. estate tax.

Owning the property through an entity may allow the investor to sidestep the estate tax issue since entities — unlike people — do not die. However, because the ratio is both subject to change and extremely dependent on each individual situation, it is important for investors to review the circumstances with a qualified CPA or cross-border tax professional to ensure that everyone understands all the ramifications. If you are buying multiple properties, there may be ways to structure the purchases in a more overall cost-effective manner.

6 — Liability

The U.S. is generally more litigious in nature than other countries. Due to this, the investor will want to ensure that he or she has adequate liability protection for both personal-use properties and investment properties. Generally speaking, investment properties involve more risk than personal properties, because other people are staying in them. Owning the property through an entity may stop your personal exposure to liability, but depending on the cash flow of the property, the holding period and other factors, there are some less expensive ways to protect the investor and his or her assets from liability risks.

7 — Cash Flow

If an investor is purchasing an investment property, he or she will want more revenues than expenses; otherwise, why would they do it? Commonly forgotten expenses include the amount of accounting and tax preparation fees. Without advance and careful planning, the cost of tax return preparation could equal any profit or gain that the investor has made. There needs to be enough cash flow to support the structure that the investor has developed. For example, a simple Limited Liability Partnership return can cost $1,200 or more. If the partnership has only one single-family home in the partnership and only grosses $1,000 per month, then you have just spent 1/12th of your gross rent simply to support your corporate structure, and you still have to file a personal tax return for each of the partners.

8 — Qualified Advice

Purchasing property in another country or state presents several challenges, not the least of which are the repercussions on the tax situation. As explained before, there are three sets of laws that you should be concerned about. The person giving the advice should have some knowledge and (preferably) experience of the three taxing authorities (U.S. tax law, Canadian tax law, U.S.-Canada tax treaty). There are too many instances of clients relying on advisors who did not fully understand this area of tax and unnecessarily incurring thousands or hundreds of thousands of dollars in professional fees, taxes and tax filings.

A common recommendation of U.S. advisors is to set up a Limited Liability Company for Canadians. From a U.S. standpoint this is a sensible recommendation, but because the U.S. advisor does not understand the Canadian tax issues, he or she may be unaware of the double tax situation created for the clients. However, a qualified cross-border advisor will be able to ask all the right questions and be able to discuss the implications on both sides of the border and prevent the adverse effects of this type of mistake.

9 — Foreign Investment in Real Property Tax Act of 1980 (FIRPTA)

Foreign Investment in Real Property Tax Act of 1980 is a law that was designed to ensure that non-resident persons who have a U.S. tax liability on appreciated U.S. real property pay these taxes. When a non-resident person (or entity) sells U.S. real property, FIRPTA requires a 25% withholding tax based on the gross selling price. However, certain forms can be filed before the close of escrow that can reduce the withholding to 25% of the gain, rather than on the sales price. Further, withholding does not apply to all sales transactions.

Often the title companies that manage the withholding do not fully understand the rules and so they apply them incorrectly. If this happens, the seller cannot get his or her money back until filing tax returns the following year. This is an area where if you do not know the rules or you do not have a qualified advisor helping you through the process, it can be difficult to get answers on the timely basis required to prevent an unnecessary loss of access to your money.

10 — Don't Let the Tax Tail Wag the Investment Dog

When purchasing U.S. property, non-U.S. persons or even U.S. residents often get so bogged down with the tax implications that they lose focus on the big picture. Taxes are important, but they are the tail of the animal that is called investing. As long as the investor has hired a qualified cross-border advisor, he or she should be able to guide you through the maze of issues to give the best tax result. You can focus on what you do best and let the referral partner help with the planning and tax advice.

Tools That are Used in Today's World to 'Find and Analyze the Deals'

There are many ways that the experienced investor has to analyze and "find" deals. And there are so many more ways that a commercial Broker can find and analyze the deals.

The commercial Broker should have access to the regional **MLS**. Big deal! So does every other Realtor. How about the knowledge to sort and drill down to the exact type of property? The MLS is like every other software computer program — the information is only as good as the person who did the inputting. Here is the other problem: Many residential agents take on the listings of multifamily or even business properties. When reviewing the numbers, often there is not a vacancy rate or property management fee on the numbers. Here are some thoughts on this: Does this mean that the owner will manage forever for nothing? Of course not; even if self-managed, the property must provide for the property management fees. What if there is no vacancy? Does this mean that the owner will guarantee that the property will always be full? Of course not, so there must always be vacancy rate in the numbers. Typically, the numbers used in the MLS are proforma and unfortunately often grossly incorrect. So be aware! Also, remember that the higher the sale price, the lower the cap rate, and in these cases the lower expenses will push the cap up. Falsely!

Loopnet is great resource. Please remember that there are many different levels of advertising that Loopnet offers and the Broker must pay the different levels for their listings. The first level is standard and if the Broker only has access to the standard level, he or she will miss many opportunities for the investor. Premium level costs money but allows the Broker access to MANY more listings.

CoStar is the granddaddy of opportunity and, frankly, is expensive to the Broker. A real commercial agent has CoStar and it is important to understand that this is equivalent to the commercial MLS.

Rentrange is another valuable source. The top 10 banks use Rentrange to value rental comparables. Ninety percent of rental comparables never hit the MLS.

Spreadsheets are another valuable tool — and in fact, not just valuable but necessary to the success of a deal. A CCIM has a spreadsheet that will evaluate both before- and after-tax values. Later in the book, we provide some examples.

A **CCIM Broker** is critical to the success of a transaction, and the reason is that they are trained to look at the entire picture, not just the front of the opportunity.

Investors often quote **Redfin, Zillow** and **Trulia** when looking at property. Remember that many commercial properties are not in their system. Their systems are usually not in real time and their comparables are almost useless, as they rely on pure square footage and not the upgrades to the properties. They can be useful in gaining an overview of the area. Unfortunately, though, not much more.

Please remember: As "they" say, **walk the dirt.** This means put your feet or your team's feet on the property. Make sure that you like the opportunity and the property.

Chapter 2
TYPES OF INVESTMENTS

Single-Family as a Good Way to Start Your Portfolio

For the first-time investor, single-family houses (SFH) can be an attractive asset to start a portfolio or add to your portfolio because oftentimes these properties can be bought for under $100,000. They are simple to maintain and easy to rent. They can cash-flow quite well for the investor. There are many ways to look at the rental income of a single-family house, but the easiest way is to use the spreadsheets that are available for investors to use. This way the investor will understand the methodology used to help decide on the property.

The benefits of using the SFH to start or diversify a portfolio come in a number of ways:

- You only have one tenant to deal with.
- The tenant usually pays all of the utilities for the property.
- You can place a home warranty on your property to cover major repairs.
- There is usually less turnover in SFH, as tenants like to sign longer leases.

Below are some criteria in looking for a SFH as a rental property:

- Newer construction (10 years of age at most)
- 3 or more bedrooms
- 2 or more bathrooms
- 2-car garage
- Tile roof
- Stucco finish
- Good rental area

- Good local schools

These factors, coupled with the team's expert rehab partners, can make your property rentable in a matter of days.

While many investors think that they can do the management for this type of investment themselves, it's always best to use a property management firm. Not only does your property management company look out for your interests, it can take care of that middle-of-the-night call about a leaking toilet. The company also will file your rental tax with the appropriate governing agencies. (Please see the section on property management.)

Multifamily Investments

Multifamily investments are often thought of as an intermediate to large investment for experienced investors only. Not so, as the experienced Broker will have the resources and ability to guide anyone through this process, and often in today's market, it makes more sense to invest in multifamily.

These types of investments are used for the investor who wants good cash flow and the benefit of depreciation. Multifamily, while typically a commercial loan product, under the Federal Tax Guidelines is still considered residential and can be fully depreciated using a 27.5-year depreciation schedule.

A Broker who specializes in multifamily is dedicated to knowing this market particularly well. The Broker should be connected directly with the multifamily brokerage world and have connections directly with the banks. With the relationships that they have built, these Brokers will usually get what is called "off-market deals," or deals that have not been advertised to the brokerage community and the general public.

What Size is Considered Multifamily?

Multifamily is usually considered to be 50-100 units, but in reality multifamily can range from duplex to an unlimited number of units. A good Broker can usually place the beginning investor into small multifamily properties (18-20 units) for about the same amount of money invested in three or four single-family homes.

For intermediate to experienced investors, there are numerous opportunities in this market. Anywhere from 20 to 500 units are attained through the use of our connections as well as our expert knowledge in working with other Brokers and the investor's commercial lenders, lawyers, inspectors, title companies and CPAs to achieve the success of the investment.

Oftentimes, the Broker is challenged with building a well-rounded portfolio for the investor. In such a case, the Broker may recommend investing in several smaller complexes that are in need of good property management and to a degree, some fixing up. It may take approximately six to nine months to complete this process. When finished, this is a very valuable tool used to either pull cash out of the building or sell and make a profit. Your commercial Broker will work with you on a long-term basis to help you, the investor, achieve these goals.

What is a Triple Net (NNN)?

A Triple Net (NNN) is a common type of lease in commercial real estate. In a NNN, the tenant is responsible for the owner's expenses, such as property taxes, maintenance and insurance. This is above and beyond the rent per square foot being charged by the owner.

With a NNN, the investor will undoubtedly work with a different commercial Broker than the one with whom he or she works on a multifamily project. It would be great if the two Brokers with separate areas of expertise were in the same office and could work together to help the investor round out his or her portfolio. A NNN as part of a diversified portfolio can work effectively for high-level investors desiring high returns and added security.

What are Some Risks Associated With a NNN Lease?

The risks of NNN leases are based on the tenant credit. A company that has a great credit rating will have a lower default rate than a company with a lower credit rating.

Owning a specialized building can be a risk, especially in a bad location, as the building might need to be improved to attract more potential tenants during a period of vacancy.

What are Some Benefits Associated With a NNN Lease?

NNN leases are longer in length than a typical residential lease, providing long-term security and potentially lowering the risk of vacancies.

Since the tenant pays all of his or her own expenses, cash flow can reliably be predicted. Tenant usage will not affect net operating income.

How Much Cash Does it Take to Invest in a NNN Lease?

NNNs start as low as $800,000 and continue into the millions. Due to the fact that commercial financing must be utilized, typically requiring 30 percent down, we can investigate a NNN investment with as little as $240,000.

What Types of Buildings are Available?

The most common NNN buildings are retail and restaurants. Almost every retail center could be considered a possibility, in addition to fast-food restaurants, large department stores and grocery stores. Offices can also be potential NNN investments.

What Kind of Businesses are Tenants in NNN Leases?

The less expensive investments will typically be smaller businesses that want to reinvest their capital in themselves rather than in real estate.

More money buys higher-end tenants, including national credit tenants, in which case the lease would be guaranteed by the corporation. Burger King, Albertsons, Wal-Mart or Starbucks are all examples of national credit tenants.

What Kind of Returns Can I Expect?

You may see a lower true cap rate, but the investor needs to think of this as either a long-term investment with long-term cash flow or the investor may be investing in a "new" shopping center that will be leased to NNN tenants. This would be considered a speculative investment, which at times can be the most profitable.

What Steps are Needed to Get Started?

The investor needs to decide on his or her long-term portfolio needs. Once this has been decided, it is now time to decide between leveraged and non-leveraged. This will determine the size of investment.

The next step is to decide if the investor wants a national tenant (usually more expensive) or a smaller type of investment. This could be a local restaurant or medical office.

The escrow is handled in much the same way as any other real estate purchase. If there are tenants in place, it is important to have a real estate attorney review the leases to make sure that not only are the leases signed correctly but that the personal guarantees are executed. This attorney should prepare estoppel agreements for the tenant to sign as well. There are some other documents that should be addressed, such as the assumption of leases, etc. These are typically either done by the title company or the attorney.

Can NNNs be Utilized in a 1031 Exchange?

Absolutely!

How Long Does the Process Take Until Closing?

There are many more areas that require close scrutiny when investing in commercial real estate. Therefore, it is preferable to allow at least 30 days to identify a short list and an additional 75 days for escrow. This is important for clients wishing to utilize a 1031 Exchange.

NNN leases are among the most solid and best-producing investments in real estate. This is due to the combination of long-term tenants with strong financials and the tenant covering the investor's expenses associated with the daily operations of the business.

There are many market factors associated with commercial real estate that require a top-tier agent representing the investor.

Fix-and-Flip or Value-Add Market

While this type of investment can be very profitable, the investor can lose a great deal of money very quickly! The real estate books tell the investor to buy a property, make a few cosmetic fixes, put it back on the market and make a huge profit.

At any given time there are half-dozen shows on television where well-dressed investors make the process look fast, fun and profitable. They don't seem to discuss the failures — and there ARE failures.

ATTOM Data Solutions reports that more than 200,000 properties in the United States were bought and resold with the same 12-month period in 2017. That's just under 6% of all the single-family properties and condominiums sold all year. Yet, the road to real-estate riches isn't all about curb appeal and "sold" signs.

The first, best piece of advice I can give is to limit the investor financial risk and also maximize investor return potential. Put simply, don't pay too much for a property (by knowing what it's worth) and make sure you also know how much the necessary repairs or upgrades will cost before buying the property. Having that information, you as the investor can then figure an ideal purchase price.

The so-called wholesalers love to say, "Here is the price, and this is the after repair value (ARV)." Their inflated numbers can be frightening.

Again, the investor needs to be really savvy about the market or have an exceptional real estate team in place to help them separate fact from fiction. This team should consist of their Broker, the construction crew and the interim financing people.

Buying multifamily is an excellent way to also look at the value-add market.

The Basics

Flipping (also called wholesale real estate investing) is a type of real estate investment strategy in which an investor purchases a property not to use, but with the intention of selling for a profit.

That profit is typically derived from price appreciation resulting from a hot real estate market in which prices are rising rapidly or from capital improvements made to the property – or both. For example, an investor might purchase a fixer-upper in a "hot" neighborhood, substantially renovate it, then offer it at a price that reflects its new state-of-the-art appearance and amenities.

Investors who flip properties concentrate on the purchase and subsequent resale of one property, or a group of properties.

So how would an investor flip a building or property? In simple terms, the investor wants to buy low and sell high (just like many other investments). But rather than adopt a buy-and-hold strategy, the investor will want to complete the renovation as quickly as possible to limit the amount of time the investor's capital is at risk. In general, the investor's focus should be on speed as opposed to maximum profit. That's because each day that passes costs the investor more money (mortgage, utilities, property taxes, insurance, etc.). It is so important to develop a plan and stick to it. If this means a larger rehab crew to cut down on the days from the beginning to the ultimate sale, so be it.

So, that's the general plan. Now, here are five common pitfalls.

Pitfall No. 1: Not Enough Money

Toying in real estate is an expensive proposition. The first expense is the property acquisition cost. While low/no-money down financing claims abound, finding these deals from a legitimate vendor is easier said than done. Also, if the investor is financing the acquisition, this means that the investor is paying interest. Although the interest on borrowed money is still tax-deductible even after the passage of the Tax Cuts and Jobs Act, it is not a 100% deduction. Every dollar spent on interest adds to the amount the investor will need to earn on the sale just to break even. And if the investor uses a mortgage or property equity line of credit (HELOC) to finance the flip-property purchase, only the interest is deductible. The principal, taxes and insurance portion of investor payments are not deductible.

Research investor financing options extensively to determine which mortgage type best suits the needs of both the investor and the property. Be sure to look at the draw process, as each lender will its own different format. Of course, paying cash for the property eliminates the cost of interest, but even then there are property holding costs and opportunity costs for tying up cash.

With interest rates having risen well off of their post-housing-crisis lows, making a profit is tougher than it used to be. In fact, the first half of 2018 saw flipping activity slow to a near four-year low and profit margins shrink to the lowest average gross return on investment (ROI) since late 2014, according to ATTOM Data. That doesn't mean there isn't money to be made (ROI was just north of 44%), but it does mean that care is required. The average gross profit on a flip is $65,520 — but that's gross.

Renovation costs must also be factored in. If the investor plans to fix the property up and sell it for a profit, the sale price must exceed the combined cost of acquisition, the cost of holding the property and the cost of renovations. A $25,000 kitchen, a $10,000 bathroom, $5,000 in real estate taxes, utilities and other carrying costs can cut that number by around two-thirds. Toss in an unexpected structural issue with the property and a gross profit can become a net loss. Even if the investor manages to overcome these hurdles, don't forget about capital gains taxes, which will chip away at the investor's profit.

Please remember to factor in your closing costs that could and probably will include commission. See the section on hold open policies.

Pitfall No. 2: Not Enough Time

Renovating and flipping properties is a time-consuming business venture. It can take months to find and buy the right property. Once investors own the property, the investor will need to invest time to fix it up. If the investor has a day job, time spent on demolition and construction can translate into lots of lost evenings and weekends. If the investor pays somebody else to do the work, he or she will still be incurring the cost of having to supervise the construction activity. Plus, the costs of paying others will reduce profit.

Is that worth it? For many people, it might make more sense to stick with a day job, where they can earn the same kind of money in a few weeks or months via a steady paycheck – with no risk and a very consistent time commitment.

Pitfall No. 3: Not Enough Skills

Professional builders and skilled professionals, such as carpenters and plumbers, often flip properties as a sideline to their regular jobs. They have the knowledge, skills and experience to find and fix a property. Some of them also have union jobs that provide unemployment checks all winter long while they work on their side projects.

The real money in property flipping comes from sweat equity — if the investor is handy with a hammer, enjoys laying carpet, can hang drywall, roof a property and install a kitchen sink. On the other hand, if the investor doesn't know a Phillips-head screwdriver from a flat screwdriver, he or she will need to pay a professional to do all of the renovations and repairs. Accordingly, the odds of making a profit on the investment will be dramatically reduced.

Pitfall No. 4: Not Enough Knowledge

To be successful, investors need to be able to pick the right property, in the right location, at the right price. In a neighborhood of $100,000 properties, does the investor really expect to buy at $60,000 and sell at $200,000? The market is far too efficient for that to occur on a frequent basis. A hot market where the returns are higher and the risk is greater costs a great deal more. The investor must be knowledgeable in the local building codes and laws as well. Pay close attention to this.

Even if the investor obtains the deal of a lifetime, snapping up a property in foreclosure for a song or from one of the local wholesalers, the investor will need to know which renovations to make and which to skip. Investors also need to understand the applicable tax laws and zoning laws and when to cut the losses and get out before the investment project becomes a money pit.

Pitfall No. 5: Not Enough Patience

Professionals take their time and wait for the right property. Novices rush out to buy the first property that they see. Then they hire the first contractor who makes a bid to address work they can't do themselves. Professionals either do the work themselves or rely on a network of pre-arranged, reliable contractors.

Professionals understand that buying and selling properties takes time and that the profit margins are sometimes slim.

The Bottom Line

Before an investor starts shopping for property, it is advisable for him or her to do some research on the nation's wealthiest individuals. The investor will quickly realize that none of them flip properties for a living. If the investor still wants to flip a property, he or she should approach the venture just as investor would any new business. And, like any other small business, the endeavor will require time and money, planning and patience, skill and effort. It will likely wind up being harder and more expensive than the investor ever imagined. And even if investors get every detail right, changing market conditions could mean that every assumption the investor made at the beginning will be invalid by the end.

Chapter 3

1031 TAX-DEFERRED EXCHANGE (FOR U.S. NATIONALS ONLY)

Why Exchange?

By electing a 1031 Exchange, certain real estate held for investment or productive use in a trade or business may qualify for the deferral of tax liability normally due on its disposition or transfer of ownership.

"No gain or loss shall be recognized on the exchange of property held for productive use in a trade or business or for investment if such property is exchanged solely for property of like kind which is to be held either for productive use in a trade or business investment." IRC §1031(a)(1).

Plain-language translation: Any gain realized on an exchange of like-kind property will not be taxed until you "cash out" of your investment.

How It All Started: Starker vs. United States

If you want to read about this landmark case, just Google it. IRC Section 1031 has been part of the IRS Code for decades upon decades! 1031 Exchange was not popular prior to this case because it was very difficult to perform until certain guidelines were put into place because of the outcome of the famous Starker Case. That is why a 1031 Exchange is commonly referred to as a "Starker Exchange." All the way back in 1967, this landmark case began the evolution of what is today IRC section 1031 Exchange. This section of the code is described in layman's terms below for your ease of use and understanding. Although the definitions and terms below are basic, IRC section 1031 when properly mastered provides for so much more than can be printed in this book, so be sure to ask!

The Basics of an Exchange

The election to do a 1031 Exchange is made by contacting (and entering into an agreement with) a Qualified Intermediary (QI) to act as a third-party facilitator. This must be done prior to the transfer of the relinquished property. To have a fully tax-deferred exchange, the exchanger should:

- Purchase "like-kind" replacement property of equal or greater value than the relinquished property
- Reinvest all of the net equity (exchange funds) from the sale of the relinquished property in the purchase of the replacement property
- Obtain equal or greater debt on the replacement property that was paid off, assumed or taken subject to the relinquished property sale

Once the relinquished property is transferred, the law allows the taxpayer 180 calendar days (or until the filing of the tax return for the year of the sale of the relinquished property, whichever comes first) to complete the acquisition of "like-kind" replacement property. All timelines begin at the time the relinquished property is transferred.

The Timelines and Identification Period

The first 45 calendar days of the Exchange are known as the Identification Period, during which the taxpayer must identify in writing to the QI what property he or she would like to have eligible for the Exchange. Even though he or she need not have the property in escrow, nor does the property have to be listed for sale, it is suggested due to the strict timeframes that negotiations should already be taking place before the 45th day. Failure to identify property by the close of business on the 45th day could void and fail the Exchange!

Identifying Properties

There are three methods for identifying property, depending on your goals in the Exchange. The taxpayer may ultimately only select one of the three methods by the 45th day. Properties on these lists may change only up to the 45th day, and no changes may be made afterward.

The three methods are:

1. The 3-Property Rule – Three properties of any value may be listed regardless of their value. One, two, or all three properties may be acquired.

2. 200% Rule – Four or more properties may be listed; however, their cumulative FMV (fair market value) may not exceed 200% of the value of the relinquished property. One or more of the properties may be acquired.

3. 95% Exception – Any number of properties of any value may be listed: however, 95% of the property MUST be purchased.

The Exchange Process

1. Exchange either at the time escrow is opened or preferably before contacting QI to discuss transaction and open the Exchange.

2. Documents are sent out to investor for review and also to the escrow company (five to seven days before COE).

3. QI coordinates with Escrow to have investor sign Exchange documents and provides escrow company with instructions for transfer of Exchange proceeds.

4. Once funds are received by the financial institution, a "receipt of funds" notification is sent to the investor along with ID documents and instructions.

5. Investor locates suitable replacement property and submits ID letter.

6. Investor opens escrow for purchase of replacement property.

7. Investor submits request for earnest money deposit funds

8. Investor submits Replacement Property Information Form with all needed information regarding the replacement property to the escrow company.

9. QI coordinates with Escrow on replacement property and obtains instructions to transfer Exchange funds to the closing of the property per the investor's desires.

10. Investor closes as normal on the property and obtains all usual documents customary in the purchase of real property.

11. Investor supplies all settlement statements and required documents to his or her CPA or tax advisor for proper reporting to the IRS.

Chapter 4
TYPES OF ENTITIES

Arizona LLC

When purchasing real estate, it is prudent for a buyer to form a limited liability company (LLC) to hold title to the property. A limited liability company is a business structure that combines the pass-through taxation of a partnership or sole proprietorship with the limited liability of a corporation. By holding title in an LLC, an owner can protect himself or herself from personal liability for the debts and obligations of the LLC. This means that if the business owes money or faces a lawsuit, only the assets of the business itself are at risk.

When choosing the state in which to form an LLC, there are several issues to consider, including taxes, where the property is located and fees.

Taxes

The LLC itself is not a separate taxable entity. Because the LLC is a pass-through entity, profits and losses pass through to the individual members of the LLC and as such, members are taxed at their individual tax rates based upon their state of domicile.

More specifically, profits and losses are allocated to each member of an LLC based upon his or her percentage of interest.

In California, the LLC is obligated to pay an annual minimum tax of $800 and a fee based on the annual total income of the LLC, in addition to the taxation on members. (This tax information is for general discussion purposes. For more information on the specific tax implications of an LLC on your individual situation, you are strongly encouraged to consult your accountant, CPA, or financial advisor.)

Where the Property is Located

If the property is located in Arizona, it is generally prudent to form the LLC in Arizona. If you form an LLC in another state (e.g., California), you will still be required to file an

Example of a Limited Liability Company Organization Chart

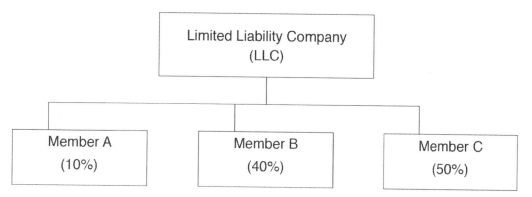

Application for Registration of a Foreign Limited Liability Company to transact business in Arizona. The expedited filing fee in Arizona is $185.

Fees

While the general filing fees for the Articles of Organization are comparable in both Arizona and California ($50 versus $70), as stated above, the State of California imposes an annual minimum tax of $800 and a fee based on the annual total income of the LLC. There are no additional annual fees for an LLC formed in Arizona.

In some instances, these additional fees alone make forming an LLC in California cost-prohibitive. As you can see, the cost of forming and maintaining an LLC in California is significantly greater than the cost in Arizona, with no corresponding benefit.

Asset Protection

When purchasing multiple properties, it is prudent for an owner to form a separate LLC to own each property. This will maximize an owner's asset protection. Separate ownership will isolate the equity in each property from potential claims brought against other properties.

For example, if multiple properties are held in one LLC and each property has $100,000 of equity, a valid claim against the LLC in excess of $100,000 would give a tenant access to the equity in the other rental properties held in the LLC not leased by the tenant with the claim.

In contrast, if a separate LLC owns each rental property, if a valid claim is received in excess of $100,000, only the property owned by that LLC is available to satisfy the tenant's claim.

Arizona LP

(It is important to understand that while limited partnerships can be formed in most states, it is necessary to choose a state to write about. Since the author lives and works in Arizona, this section will speak to Arizona.)

An Arizona LP is not complicated, but should be formed by a real estate attorney, as there are many moving parts. In addition, for Canadian investors purchasing real estate in Arizona, LP is the preferred ownership entity for both liability protection and tax purposes.

The LP consists of both general partners and limited partners. The general partners have authority under Arizona law to enter into contracts and conduct the business of the partnership, while the limited partners are most often treated as passive investors but may be given more authority as to major decisions of the partnership. There are potential security considerations involving limited partnerships, so great care should be taken in how you form the partnership.

The general partner of a limited partnership is generally (i.e., personally) liable for the debts of the partnership, while the limited partners' liability is limited to the assets of the partnership. As a result, the creation of an LP used for real estate investment usually involves the inclusion of a general partner that, while it manages the LP, has a very nominal stake in the LP, usually 1% or less. Typically, the general partner is also a single purpose entity (SPE), which has as its only function running the LP. The effect of this structure is that the GP has very minimal liability; while the GP may remain personally liable for the debts of the LP, the GP holds little interest in the LP and has no real assets as an SPE.

You are strongly encouraged to consult an attorney in creating the partnership to ensure you are not running afoul of state securities laws, and that the partnership is properly formed to protect you from liability.

In addition, the LP provides for partnership tax treatment, which is not available to Canadian investors in any other entity form. Under partnership tax treatment, profits and losses are "passed through" the entity to its partners for tax purposes, rather than being taxed at the entity level and personal level, as for instance, a corporation would be taxed. The partners then individually pay taxes on their allocable profits and gain the benefit of their allocable losses. By using an entity form that allows for pass-through taxation, a Canadian investor can avoid double taxation that would result from paying taxes once individually in the U.S., and then a second time at the capital gains rate in Canada.

For more information about the taxation of a Canadian Investor, you are strongly encouraged to consult your Chartered Accountant (CA) or other qualified tax professional.

Typically, an LP can be formed in Arizona within 10 business days. Since the LP affords personal liability protection, it is highly recommended that the property be closed in the name of the new entity. However, it may not be possible to take title in the LP at the time of closing, in which case you are advised to seek counsel to properly transfer title while retaining your title insurance and preserving your loan agreement.

Additionally, in order to minimize your liability, it is recommended that you use a separate LP for each property.

Chapter 5
INSURANCE

Rehab Insurance

Rehab insurance is one of the more important and complex types of insurance to deal with when buying a property. Most insurance companies won't write insurance for properties undergoing renovation work.

Investment properties requiring renovation present risks for the insurer due to contractors coming and going, as well as the threat of vandalism and theft. It is important to find a policy that will cover the property while it is vacant and under renovation. The type of renovation work that is happening will also dictate the type of policy that will be needed. The more extensive the rehab, the more extensive the policy will have to be.

Normal renovation policies last anywhere from one month to one year because the owner usually is going to try to sell the property. The insurance company is well aware of this and thus charges higher premiums and also sometimes has minimum earned premiums on the policies. At the end of the day, these types of policies will be about 40%-50% more expensive than standard landlord/tenant-occupied policies because of the risks that come with renovating a home.

Buy-and-Hold Policies

When it comes to insurance, policies for buy-and-hold properties is fairly standard. Usually buy-and-holds are properties that will either have a quick rehab (30 days or less) to fix up some cosmetic issues and then find a tenant to occupy it, or they are already tenant-occupied. In either instance, the investor will need a landlord policy (Dwelling Fire 3) that covers the property. This policy will protect the inside and outside structure of the home from potential claims of fire, wind, hail, theft, water, etc. There are options to add additional coverage on these policies; for example, to cover for code upgrades that might be needed after a claim and also to cover any personal property the owner of the home has inside the property (more than likely that will only be appliances).

Liability Insurance for LLC or LP

With any property, there is always the opportunity to title the property in the name of an LLC or LP. From an insurance perspective, using an entity is extremely beneficial, as it limits the amount of personal exposure there is to an individual's assets if there was a physical damage or liability claim at the property.

I always tell clients to consult with an attorney about this, as attorneys are very knowledgeable about the pros and cons of using an entity. As far as the cost of insurance and/or insurability, it has become more popular than ever to use an entity and does not affect premiums or coverages on a policy if an entity is being used.

Extra Note on Insurance

Insurance doesn't cover every single thing that happens at a property. There are certain exclusions that every policy carries. Insurance policies also don't cover maintenance items or wear and tear, as it is still the property owner's responsibility to maintain and repair the property as needed when items are getting old.

Insurance is there to protect against the sudden and unexpected!

Chapter 6
TITLE & ESCROW

Life of an Escrow

1. Opening the Escrow

- Assemble the items needed to open escrow:
    - Fully executed Purchase Contract (including any counters and addendums)
    - Earnest money deposit
    - Copy of listing agreement
    - New lender information
    - Existing loan payoff information
    - Buyer and seller information
    - Real estate Broker information for buyer and seller
    - Rent rolls and copies of all leases

2. Processing the Escrow

- Escrow deposits earnest money funds.
- Escrow orders Preliminary Title Report from title department.
- Escrow requests payoff or assumption information, homeowner's association information, etc.

3. Title Examination

- Property and parties are researched by the title examiner.
- Preliminary Title Report is typed and sent to escrow officer, agents, seller and buyer.

4. Escrow Closing Preparation

- Preliminary Title Report received by escrow officer, who reviews for any surprises (i.e., tax liens, judgments, unknown liens of record, discrepancies in legal description, delinquent taxes, access problems, etc.).
- Escrow advises agents if additional information is needed to clear any surprises revealed by the Preliminary Title Report.
- Escrow follows up on receipt of the following if needed, per Purchase Contract:
  » Termite report
  » Home protection plan
  » Buyer's hazard insurance
  » New loan package
  » Payoff information
  » Repair bills
  » Warranties
- Loan documents are received, and the escrow officer "works" the file to reflect closing and advises agents of funds that are needed for closing.
- Closing appointment times are set for seller and buyer with escrow officer.
- All parties executing documents are advised to bring a valid government-issued picture I.D. (driver's license, passport, etc.).
- Buyer (or seller) advised to bring in a cashier's check or wired funds for closing.

5. Execution of Documents

- Buyer and seller meet with escrow officer and execute all documents (certainly this can be done with a notary; however, this must be with a Title-approved notary).

6. Lender's Funds

- After all parties have executed the necessary documents, Escrow returns the loan package to new lender for review and funding.
- Lender funds the loan and lender's check or wired funds are sent to Escrow for processing.

7. Recordation

- After Escrow receives all funds needed and has ascertained that conditions are met, original documents are recorded. Once documents are recorded, Escrow notifies agents.

- Agents will make arrangements for you to transition the property to the property management company.

8. Disbursement of Funds
- All disbursements are made in accordance with the settlement statement.

9. Policies Issued
- Purchaser receives owner's title Insurance policy from the title company.
- New lender receives ALTA loan policy from the title company.

What is a Closing Protection Letter and What Does it Protect Buyer/Seller From?

A Closing Protection Letter specifically applies to escrow closing activities and services performed by approved agents who provide title policies on behalf of title insurers. It protects against fraud, defalcation, or the failure of an agent to follow written instructions given by the principals of the transaction (i.e., lender instructions, purchase contract).

These letters are standardized indemnity agreements given to buyer, seller and/or new lender upon request and recite the specific conditions under, and the extent to which, title underwriters will accept liability for the acts or omissions of a settlement agent.

Question:
Does the closing protection letter issued to the new lender protect the buyer/borrower?

Answer:
It does not. For the buyer/borrower to enjoy the same protection, they need to request a CPL in their name.

Question:
Is there an additional cost to request a Closing Protection Letter?

Answer:
Yes, there is, and it varies from title insurer to title insurer, ranging on average from $5 to $25.

Critical Date Letter

Managing the dates and deadlines of the contract is one of the most important (albeit unglamorous) tasks of the Broker, Title and Escrow, the lender and, of course, the investor. Missing a critical deadline could have far-reaching implications. The Critical Date Letter is used to guide everyone through the process, to easily manage important tasks and deadlines all in one place. A Critical Date Letter can be created for either a residential or a commercial transaction.

When the contract is sent to the title company, it is the escrow or title person's responsibility to provide a Critical Date Letter according to the terms and conditions of the contract. When this is received, it is essential that all parties take a good look at the timeline dates. The real estate Brokers or attorneys who have negotiated the contract should make sure that they agree with the dates as well. This is the time to be sure that Title and Escrow understand and that everyone is on the same page. The buyer and seller also need to be sure that they understand and comply with the dates. And the lender needs to be on board.

If there are dates that are not right, the escrow company can change this easily and recirculate the document. If the contract changes with a written addendum signed by the buyer and seller, there will need to be a new Critical Date Letter issued. Remember that the dates go by the contract, counters and addendums and that only these items can change the dates. Also, do not simply rely on the Critical Date Letter, as this is the title company's interpretation of the contract, so read very carefully.

Explanation of a Preliminary Title Report

Schedule A on a title report is similar to an accounting of "the basics," and the items can be changed in a few seconds by the title company. Schedule B includes items that are considered "clouds" on title and must be cleared prior to the close of escrow. Often, the escrow officer and agent are already working on these matters even before the investor will see this.

Here are some tips and other items to help you understand and navigate the process:

• Check the name of the buyer and seller. If this is going to be changed to an entity later, that is OK; it can be done as soon as the entity documents are provided to the title company for review.

• It is REALLY important if the investor is taking title as sole and separate property in a community property state, that it is clearly defined. Additionally, if the investor is married, this also should be clearly stated. The spouse can provide a disclaimer deed (which will need to be notarized) prior to close. In situations where there is a divorce or legal separation in the works, this can be handled in the same way.

- If the sales price changes, this also can be amended in a few minutes.
- If there is a lender involved, the lender will be named. If you are using a mortgage broker, the actual lending institution will be the entity that is named.
- Title will supply the legal description of the property. The investor will probably not see the address on the title commitment.

Following are typical entries found on Schedules A and B:

Schedule A

- Commitment No.: Escrow Number
- Commitment Amount:
  » Owner's $ Based on Sales Price
  » Lender's $ Based on Mortgage Amount
- Name of Proposed Insured
- Lender: Bank issuing new mortgage
- Owner: In a sale, owner provides the policy to the buyer
- Your interest in land covered by this policy will be:
- Fee Simple: An estate of inheritance without limitation to any particular class of heirs and with no restrictions upon alienation. Sometimes known as fee simple absolute, the largest interest or estate in real property a person may own.
- Upon issuance of policy fee title will be vested in: i.e.,
  » John G. Smith and Susan L. Smith, husband and wife
  » John G. Smith, an unmarried man
  » Susan L. Smith, a single woman
  » Susan L. Smith, wife of John G. Smith, as her sole and separate property (When a married person takes title as sole and separate owner, a quitclaim deed is required)
- The entity name and the kind of entity
- The land referred to in this commitment is described as follows: Legal description of property

Schedule B

- Taxes for required part of the year (In Arizona and many states these are paid in arrears and always appear here. However, all property taxes must be current as of the Close of Escrow.)

- Any changes upon said land by reason of inclusion in homeowner's association of unit owner's association as more fully disclosed in Covenants, Conditions and Restrictions (CC&Rs)** set forth below. These are often shown as a link to an online document, and it is important to click on any links and read the documents.

- **CC&Rs — Limitations sometimes put on the use and enjoyment of real property. This can be done with agreements contained in deeds and other documents.

- Water rights, claims or title to water, whether or not the matters expected are shown by public records

- An easement** and rights incident thereto for electric lines and appurtenant facilities, over said premises, as set forth in instrument recorded in Document No. XXX

There are almost always, at the minimum, utility easements on property. Remember that if the investor plans to add to the property — even a pool, these must be explored.

- An easement and rights incident thereto for cable television service and maintenance agreement, as set forth in instrument recorded in Document No. XX-XXXXX

- All matters contained in the Covenants, Conditions, Restrictions, Easement, Liens and Charges, as set forth in instrument recorded in Document No. XX-XXXXXX

This is the section that has to be worked and each requirement must be met prior to closing.

Sometimes when the investor has a common name, an identity statement clears the judgments and perhaps liens prior to close of escrow. The title company typically sends to the buyer and seller an opening letter, which contains the identity statement. It is critically important that this be filled out and returned to the title company early in escrow in order to clear these requirements. Also, in the event of a valid lien, the buyer or seller will need to work with Title and the lien holder to clear this early.

- Commitment No.: Escrow Number Requirements:

    » Payment of taxes for the first or second half of the year, depending on the date of closing

    » Record satisfaction, in full, of judgments or liens which show up in public records

» Proper showing that all assessments due and payable, levied by the Homeowner's Association (an Arizona non-profit corporation) have been paid to and including the closing date of this transaction

» Record Release and Reconveyance Deed of Trust executed by (i.e., John G. Smith, an unmarried man), as Trustor, to (lender) as beneficiary dated (closing), recorded on (date) in Document No XXXXXXX; and thereafter assigned to (name of current loan servicer), by assignment recorded (date) in Document No. XX)00(XX. Amount: Mortgage Amount)

» Record Deed of Trust as set forth in Schedule B

Title Insurance

Most consumers do not fully understand what title insurance is for or what it covers. They do understand that it is needed to close a real estate transaction and that a seller pays for an owner's title insurance policy for a buyer and a buyer pays for a lender policy for their lender if a buyer requires financing.

What title insurance really provides is peace of mind to consumers and lenders. The primary purpose of title insurance is to protect an insured from financial loss as well as loss of use and enjoyment of real estate.

In a typical real estate sale transaction, there are two title insurance policies required:

- An owner's title insurance policy, which a seller provides to the buyer insuring that the buyer will have clear title to the property that they are purchasing
- A lender's title insurance policy, which insures clear title to the lender that is providing financing.

Title insurance provides protection against past events, unlike most insurance products which focus on insuring against possible future events. The premium paid for title insurance is a one-time payment, whereas most insurance premiums are paid annually. The owner's title Insurance policy is usually issued in the amount of the real estate sales price and the lender's title insurance policy is usually issued in the amount of the new loan. Consumers and lenders are also able to purchase additional title insurance, called endorsements, which are similar to a rider to a homeowner's insurance policy.

When someone is in the process of buying or selling a property, a title company will search the public records and review the ownership history, looking at deeds, deeds of trust, releases, liens, judgments and so forth that would affect the title insurance company's ability to provide clear title.

Some of the most common risks that title insurance policies protect against are:

CHAPER 6 — TITLE & ESCROW

- Deeds, deeds of trust and wills that contain improper vesting and incorrect names
- Outstanding mortgages, judgments and tax liens
- Easements
- Improper notary acknowledgements
- Mistakes in recording of documents
- Liens for unpaid property taxes
- Forgeries
- Fraud
- Undisclosed heirs
- Deeds by persons of unsound mind

It is really important to discuss here the use of the quitclaim deed. This clearly breaks the chain of title and may very well void the title insurance that is on the property. A quitclaim deed is a deed like no other. It's a quick and easy form that can be completed in five minutes to transfer real property. But despite its many advantages, quitclaims do not work well for every real estate transaction. These deeds make no guarantees about the property interest being transferred or about liens or other encumbrances on the property. If the investor is moving title to another person or entity and that person or entity has judgments or liens, they WILL attach to the property. So be very careful about quitclaim deeds and consult a real estate attorney before using one.

In order to remove someone's interest off of the property, a disclaimer deed is used. This states that the person relinquished his or her interest in the property. Even if the property owner used a quitclaim deed and then a disclaimer deed, this will NOT undo the error, and the judgments or liens will still stay with the property.

I was once involved in a case in which the seller thought they could avoid foreclosure by using a quitclaim deed to a friend, and guess what?

This person had over a hundred thousand dollars of liens. The property was only worth about a hundred thousand and had a mortgage on it already. This not only made the title not warrantable or sellable without the seller bringing into the closing all of these funds, but it also actually forced the seller into bankruptcy. Any competent attorney, title company or real estate broker would have told this person that this was a horrible idea. Had this action been taken through the title company — which with the mortgage it really could not have been done — the title company would have seen the judgments and stopped this situation from happening. Please remember that the title cannot be changed using title insurance without the full knowledge of the lender or other lien holders.

In reverse, if a person or entity was quitclaimed onto a title and the existing owner had judgments or liens, the new person or entity has now opened themselves up to the existing problems as well.

Hold Open Policies and Why They are Needed

If an investor plans on renovating a property and reselling the property to a third party in less than two years, he or she has the option to obtain a hold open policy from a title insurance company. These policies must be paid for at the time that a consumer purchases a property and are typically an additional charge of 25% of the basic owner's policy rate. The seller on a real estate transaction typically pays for the buyer's owner's insurance policy. The buyer would be responsible for the additional 25% premium. Upon close of escrow, the buyer will then have one to two years (sometimes up to four) to sell the subject property and close out their hold open policy. (Terms and costs vary by title insurance underwriter for hold open policies and the time period can sometimes be extended for an additional time period for an additional fee paid prior to the expiration of the initial hold open period.)

Why would an investor do this? It simply means that the investor who was the buyer and now becomes the seller will only be paying for the new owner's policy difference between the original purchase price and the new purchase price. It can and has saved investors hundreds, if not thousands, of dollars. It is important to note that when the property is sold and it goes into escrow, the same title company must do the second escrow, as they have the hold open policy.

Many agents and even some Brokers do not know about this option. When a property is listed for sale and there is a hold open policy, it should be disclosed to the potential buyers and buyer's agents. This does NOT mean, as is often said, that the buyer's title company will offer investor rates or "match" the seller's title company's fees. This is not the same thing, and many times the listing Broker will need to kindly educate the buyer's agent on this.

A hold open policy means that a title insurance company will not issue the owner's title insurance policy to the buyer at the closing of the initial real estate transaction. Instead they will hold it open until the property has been sold and will then issue the owner's title insurance policy to the ultimate purchaser.

The reason an investor would want to purchase a hold open policy is that there would be considerable cost savings when the property is subsequently sold to the ultimate purchaser, as the title premium charged on the second transaction would be substantially less. The owner's title insurance policy is the greatest fee charged by a title insurance company in a real estate transaction, as it is based on the sales price and presumably the sales price will be greater in the buyer's (now seller's) sale to the end buyer, resulting in greater savings.

It is important to note that with a hold open policy, the title insurance policy is not completely issued until this is closed. What happens if at the expiration period the subject property has not closed? The owner (investor) either can extend the hold open policy or he or she will need to contact the title company and request that they close the policy (and this is when they actually issue the title insurance policy). While this sounds complicated, it really is not.

Chapter 7
PROPERTY MANAGEMENT

Property Management is Not for Everyone

Property management is not for everyone! If the investor has a full-time day job that's not real estate investing, he or she should seriously consider hiring a professional management company to take care of the investment.

Dealing with tenants is not everyone's cup of tea. Even if the investor does real estate investing full-time, consider how much your time is worth and then see how valuable a management company truly is and how much it frees up the investor to do what he or she does best. It is recommended that an investor use property management with any real estate buy-and-hold strategy.

Not all property managers are the same. A property manager shouldn't just collect the rent payments. Other services such as bookkeeping, handling move-ins and move-outs, maintenance, marketing and legal services should also be included.

Advantages of using a professional management company

Any property manager can collect rent, but the best property managers will collect other income generated by sources such as laundry, vending, utility and maintenance repairs. On the flip side, management of expenses also should be the responsibility of the property manager, such as vendor costs, deferred maintenance costs and lease renewals.

Bookkeeping

Monthly cash flow statements, operating statements, general ledger management, check detail, rent roll, bank reconciliations and copies of all invoices should be provided. Some companies offer a web-based program that will allow owners to access their account from anywhere in the world 24 hours a day, seven days a week.

Marketing

Marketing plans developed by a property manager will help determine the occupancy results at your property. By creating curb appeal, generating word of mouth and marketing via signage, classifieds, real estate agents and using a referral system from "sister" properties, a property manager can keep the vacancy rate at your property low.

Tenant Screening

A property manager should pre-qualify prospective residents by making sure applications are properly and completely filled out, past residential and current job verifications are completed and credit and background checks are done. This service will make sure the prospective resident meets the minimum qualifications necessary.

Legal Issues

Having a resource for legal services is another reason to utilize a property management company. One that can serve various notices from a "5-day notice to pay rent or quit" to a "30-day notice to vacate" and everything in between is the ideal solution.

Repairs and Maintenance

Management of minor to major repairs can be completed by a property management company. A good property manager is one that can receive and negotiate bids for large projects and will discuss the options with you to provide the highest quality at the lowest price. Daily minor maintenance issues that require the services of electricians, landscapers, locksmiths, painters, plumbers and more should also be included.

With all of this in mind, the Broker should maintain close working relationships with the very best property management companies. This is just another advantage of using an experienced Broker to reach your investment goals.

What are the Duties of a Property Manager?

Property managers need to have had a solid background in operations management, technology, sales and the ability to deal with people of all kinds. Investors have heard the horror stories of property management. There are times when investors cannot believe the issues that arise in the day-to-day duties of the property management.

LINDA GERCHICK'S PRACTICAL GUIDE TO COMMERCIAL REAL ESTATE

Here is a list showing the usual responsibilities of a property manager:

- Agent to the seller
- Register the property as a rental property with either the state or county, listing the new ownership and property management company
- Apply for the rental tax license
- Prepare units for rent
- Market properties for lease
- Perform move-in and move-out inspections
- Receive and screen tenant applications
- Pay bills for owners
- Turn utilities on and off
- Sign leases

- Collect monies
- Collect debts
- Maintain investment property
- Serve as administrator for property management software
- Business development
- Law enforcement
- Psychiatrist
- Comedian
- Marriage counselor

There are times when tenants do not like property managers to call about their late rent payments. Who likes to speak to a debt collector? However, it is the function of the property manager to make the call on behalf of the owner. They work for the owner.

One can see that a property manager has to wear many hats. It is important to have a property manager to balance the relationship between the tenant and owner's interests.

Overall, there is a lot to do in this business. There is never a boring day.

Transition into Property Management

A good agent and a good property management company need to work together even after the close of escrow to make the transition to the property manager an easy process. This is done with good communication and sharing of information. If the owner and property manager have decided that the current tenants are going to be retained, the transition and communication must be fluid. Many companies make this a complicated process, especially if the current property manager is being replaced with another one.

First, the owner and the property owner sign the management agreement, laying out the contract terms, dates and signatures of both parties. It is important to note that if the new owner is taking ownership in an entity that ALL new leases be created with the entity as the landlord, rather than listing the owner's personal name. This also includes that property management agreement.

The property manager will send out notices to the tenants to inform them of the change in property management and where to either mail the rent checks or often giving the tenants access to a tenant portal where they can pay rent and also report any maintenance issues.

The property manager will need to coordinate with the agent to ensure that utility accounts are changed at close of escrow. They also need to see that they change all utilities so there is no disruption in service to the tenants. In addition, the property manager will need to notify any service providers of either a discontinuation or change of billing. If there is a coin-operated laundry room or vending machines, the property manager will need to notify the company of where to send the income from this service.

As with the tenant portals, property management companies use software that also provide owners with their own portals. The property company should help the owner set up his or her portal. This portal should have copies of all current leases, an accurate rent roll, the income and expenses for the property. Do not accept a charge that says simply "plumbing repair;" the investor should have access to the actual invoice through the portal. The books and records should be clear and easy to understand. If that is not the case, interact with whomever is in charge of the bookkeeping so that it becomes clear and easy to understand.

There are some items that are critical for the property manager to set up in order to maintain the investor's property or properties. Much of the following information can be handled among the agent, escrow and property management; whatever is not supplied should be provided to the property manager by the owner as soon as possible.

Security deposits are not the property of either the owners or of the property management company. They should be transferred at close of escrow to the property management company, who by law must place these in their trust account. This is for the safekeeping of the tenant's security deposits. After the tenant moves out and any damages are accounted for, the security deposits are then disbursed either to the tenant or to the owner's account.

While different property management companies vary in their requirements, here are some of the basics:

- LLC or LLLP information — This means all the paperwork including operating agreements and a W-9 (this is so the property management company can pay the investor's income)
- Owner's name, mailing address, phone and email (if the investor moves at any time or changes any of the above, please notify the property management company ASAP)
- Emergency contact information
- Mortgage information
- Insurance information
- HOA/CCRs information
- Tenant/vendor leases
- Home warranty information

CHAPTER 7 — PROPERTY MANAGEMENT

- Keys
- Banking information — If using an entity it will need to be the entity bank account.
- Tenant applications
- Tenant contact information
- Any plans for rehab or renovation
- Security deposits

Transaction Privilege Tax for Rentals

Many municipalities require the owner (via the property management company) to pay a "rental tax" on the rent collected. Since I practice in Arizona, I am going to speak for Arizona, but it is critical that the owner understand these laws wherever the property is located.

It is hard to believe that many real estate investors who own and rent out real estate in Arizona have never heard of transaction privilege tax (TPT), but it is true. More understandable is that most renters also are unaware of this tax. The best thing property managers can do is to educate both landlords and tenants on TPT.

What is TPT? It is simply a tax on the monthly rent that must be collected and paid to the State of Arizona. The amount paid in rental sales tax depends on where the rental unit is in Arizona. Each Arizona city imposes a different tax rate.

Investors and Tenants

The owner — not the tenant — is responsible for paying the TPT on the property, but the total rent charged for a property can be calculated to cover this expense. A good property manager states the TPT disclosed rate and the amount directly on the lease.

Consider this example:

123 N 1st Avenue Phoenix, AZ 850001. Rent: $900 monthly.

The TPT tax in Phoenix as of this writing is 2.3%. The monthly TPT for this property will be $20.70. Total rent plus TPT monthly collected from tenant will be $920.70. Then, the property management pays the $20.70 to the state on the investor's behalf. This is called a pass-through expense, and while it is important to have this, just imagine losing 2.3% of your profit or bottom line due to the property manager not collecting this from the tenant.

County Assessor Residential Rental Registration

All Arizona counties require all residential properties to be registered with the County

Assessor. There are some investors who keep the status as residential but still rent the property to a tenant, so they do not have to pay taxes. However, an owner can expect heavy penalties and fines for properties that are not clearly identified as a rental property with the County Assessor.

Here is the question to real estate investors: Is it worth it to be a fraud? It is always best to follow the law.

How Much is the TPT?

Every city has its own TPT rate. Please visit the Arizona Department of Commerce to research the different rates depending on the location of the rental property.

Leave it to the Experts

In my opinion, it is best to hire a professional property management company. Be sure that the person at the property management company supplies the investor the reports showing that the rental tax has been paid.

Business License

Some cities in Arizona make a landlord/property management company obtain a business license. Please refer to the Arizona Department of Commerce for further information.

Penalty for Not Paying TPT

This is a great resource of income for many Arizona cities. There are cities that have developed a whole separate department for collecting back taxes from landlords. The bottom line is that the cities want their money — with no excuses. Owners will start paying late fees and other fines imposed by the state for nonpayment of TPT.

It is always best to stay compliant with Arizona state agencies.

Capital Expenditure

A capital expenditure is simply something the investor can capitalize over a period of time — over a year or more. It adds value to the current property, and it is normally a one-time major expense such as installing a new HVAC unit. Please review the table on the next page showing examples of capital expenditures vs. maintenance repairs.

Capital vs. Maintenance Budget

When investing in real estate, you will need to set up two budgets: a capital budget (often called a reserve budget) and a maintenance budget.

The maintenance budget will be used to maintain the property by paying for such things

CAPITAL EXPENDITURE	MAINTENANCE REPAIR
Install new AC units	Repair the AC unit
Install new doors	Paint a bedroom
Install a new roof	Repair the garbage disposal
Install new electrical panels	Repair the kitchen sink leak
Install new double pane windows	Repair roof leak
Install new hot water heater	Landscape clean up
Install new plumbing piping	Remove debris from the property
Install new plumbing fixtures	Repair hose bib
Install a new pool	New window pane
Erect a block fence around the property	
Install new appliances	
Install solar panels	
Install new sewer system for property	

as removal of trash, water leaks, HVAC repairs, fan replacement and other incidental repairs needed to maintain the property for current tenants.

A capital budget will be utilized for expenditures listed on the left-hand side of the accompanying chart. These are one-time major expenditures that are needed on the property such as installing a new HVAC unit. It is vital for an investor to have capital reserves in case an owner must install a new roof in an emergency. An investor will create a capital expenditure plan and implement it to increase the property's value over a period of time.

If the investor is acquiring a commercial loan, the commercial lender will require a capital reserve. Usually, this is $250 per unit, but it can be more. This capital reserve fund is held by the bank in an escrow account.

Let's say that the property needs a new parking lot. The investor usually has to install the parking lot and then get reimbursed by the bank from the escrow account.

When we speak of Chattel or cost segregation, this is considered accelerated depreciation. This is used to offset passive income and is very valuable at tax time.

It is important to understand that capital expenditures are not operating expenses. The books and records need to reflect this at sale time. Wouldn't it be a shame to have missed a potential buyer because the operating expenses had an extra $5,000 in it for a new air conditioner that should have been categorized as a capital expense? Whereas many potential buyers might pass on a deal, the savvy Broker and investor can look at the books and records and choose to accept the deal, as they recognize that the capital vs. operating numbers may be off.

Finally, it is always recommended that an investor align himself or herself with a tax professional who is familiar with real estate — one who not only understands but will take the time to use the Chattel to maximize the investor's annual tax returns.

Real estate is a great way to obtain wealth. Let's be a part of something bigger than oneself.

Rent Rolls and Their Importance in Real Estate Investing

A rent roll is a snapshot of rents due for the period as confirmed on valid leases. The rent roll is utilized by owners, property managers, lending institutions and any other party involved to understand the value and performance of a real estate asset. Rent rolls are essential to monitor for two great reasons:

1. Track the performance of the asset
2. Track the performance of the property management company

You will see the following information on a current roll:

- Address and unit number
- Square footage of unit

- Tenant's name
- Start date and end date of lease
- Rent amount
- Last date paid rent
- Security deposit on hold
- Paid rent vs. monies owed
- Total rent paid vs. total still outstanding
- Vacancies
- Number of bedrooms and bathrooms

The rent roll is the most vital instrument utilized when determining the value of an income property. Hence, it is vital that the property management accounting is always immaculate. Certifying the numbers on the rent roll with the current leases in place leads to a high comfort level for an investor that the asset has been properly managed prior to his or her purchase of it. This is part of the due diligence granted when purchasing real estate to ensure that all the numbers add up and the current leases in place are valid.

Rent rolls are highly desirable in commercial real estate for analyzing real estate deals. Rent rolls are used for the following reasons:

- Calculate annual rental revenue
- Identify the performance of the asset
- Opportunity to increase property performance
- Identify tenants receiving rent concessions
- Count tenants who are month-to-month

A solid rent roll and a trailing 12-month operating statement are vital for any lending institution to underwrite a deal.

Landlord's Responsibility When it Comes to Federal Fair Housing

So, the investor has a property management company, and while he or she may think that their property manager will comply with all federal and state laws — especially when it comes to Fair Housing and disabilities — this may not always be the case. If the property manager fails to follow these laws, it is extremely likely that the owner or the landlord will be brought to action as well.

Landlords have a broad latitude when choosing new residents based on their credit scores, criminal history, financial ability to pay and renting history. However, there are limitations imposed by the U.S. federal government regarding an applicant's personal characteristics that must not be a factor when making a decision.

The Fair Housing Act's protected classes, described in the provisions of the Fair Housing Act, can be a source of confusion, giving rise to problems in certain situations. It is important to follow federal regulations when leasing the properties to prospective tenants.

The property manager and the landlord must strictly adhere to all requirements of the Fair Housing laws that state it is illegal to discriminate against any person in the protected classes.

Title VIII of the Civil Rights Act of 1968 (Fair Housing Act), as amended, prohibits discrimination in the sale, rental and financing of dwellings, and in other housing-related transactions, based on race, color, national origin, religion, sex, familial status (including children under the age of 18 living with parents or legal custodians, pregnant women, and people securing custody of children under the age of 18), and disability.

Prohibited Actions

Property management companies and landlords will not discriminate against any applicant for reasons of race, color, creed, national origin, sex, age, marital status, familial status, or physical or mental disability.

Examples of prohibited actions based on renting to protected classes are:

- Refusal to rent housing
- Refusal to negotiate for housing
- Making housing unavailable
- Advertising for a specific group of people
- Setting different terms, conditions or privileges for rental
- Denying a visually impaired tenant the exception to keep a guide dog in a dwelling with a "no pets" policy

The property manager must display the Fair Housing poster, as required. Failure to do so is deemed a discriminatory housing practice and prima facie evidence of a violation of the Fair Housing Act.

In other words, not having the poster up is illegal, and if someone accuses the property manager of discrimination, lack of the poster could be taken as presumptive evidence that they were guilty of discrimination.

Clearly, any rental-housing provider's failure to post the mandated Equal Housing Opportunity Poster, or a reasonable facsimile, would put himself or herself in jeopardy of having to defend a Fair Housing complaint, filed by anyone.

Therefore, the HUD Fair Housing poster should be placed at a conspicuous place in the rental office for all to see upon entry. Any person who feels they are injured by a housing provider's violation of the poster requirement could file a complaint of discrimination.

Disabilities

In essence, a landlord may not:

- Refuse to let a disabled person make reasonable modifications to the dwelling or common use areas, at their expense, if necessary for the disabled person to use the housing. (Where reasonable, the landlord may permit changes only if the disabled person agrees to restore the property to its original condition when they move.)

- Refuse to make reasonable accommodations in rules, policies, practices or services if necessary for the disabled person to use the housing.

Example: An apartment complex that offers tenants ample, unassigned parking must honor a request from a mobility-impaired tenant for a reserved space near her apartment if necessary to assure that she can have access to her apartment.

Routine Maintenace in Property Management

Owning real estate is a contact sport, in my opinion. One must always be able to deal with people and have a preventive maintenance program in place in order to avoid huge repairs down the road. Many do-it-yourself landlords only focus on collecting the monthly rent and only do repairs when the tenants report them. However, what about the constant water leaking in the toilet where the owner pays for the water? It is always best to be proactive when it comes to maintenance on a property vs. major repairs down the road.

So many times, when inspections are done, many major repair issues are uncovered and the tenant will say over and over, "I was going to tell you."

Game Plan Routine Maintenance

Here are some ways to be proactive when it comes to maintenance:

- Send out quarterly surveys to tenants asking them if there are any maintenance issues at the current residence. Admittedly, water can cause a lot of damage if not addressed immediately.

- Property manager conducts a drive-by monthly (or other regular) inspection in the area. The property manager can then schedule any item that appears to be out of place on the exterior, such as a broken window or roof shingles loose or missing, to name a few examples.

- Conduct annual inspections on the property when a lease is up for renewal or conduct a move-out inspection.

- Place a unit on a preventive maintenance schedule to ensure things are being completed on the property without relying on the tenant.

- One of the items that is proactive and nonintrusive to the tenant is "changing the filters" every quarter. This allows the maintenance staff to go into the unit and "see" items or tenant noncompliance with leases (such as unauthorized tenants or unauthorized pets).

Charge Back Tenant for Repairs

There are times when the tenant should be charged immediately for repairs due to their error. A good example would be that of a tenant who breaks a glass cup in the sink and clogs the sink. The plumber repairs the issue. The tenant is charged back, as this tenant caused the problem. This is an item that should be addressed in the lease. The tenant – not the owner – should pay the bill. In my experience, many property managers side with the tenant and not the owner in order to keep the peace. But remember: The property manager works for the owner and not for the tenant.

Recommended Schedule of Maintenance

MONTHLY ITEMS

- Check AC filter to prevent HVAC issues
- Run dishwasher to avoid still-water issues
- Flush toilets to make sure they run properly
- Make sure all locks function
- Are all light switches working?
- Do garage door openers operate?

ANNUAL ITEMS

- Full service on HVAC in the springtime before summer weather
- Flush hot water heaters to remove sediment and ensure longer use

- Test smoke detectors
- Check all water areas to ensure no leaks (both interior and exterior)
- Examine all windows
- Examine the exterior roof
- Check all window blinds to ensure they function properly
- Inspect all interior and exterior doors
- Test all appliances
- Walk the entire perimeter of the property
- Inspect the roof to ensure no loose shingles or debris
- Make sure no tree branches are touching the roof
- Check for cockroaches or other pest-control issues
- Examine shower caulking and grout between the tiles
- Clean gutters

Benefits of a Proactive Preventive Maintenance Plan

- Avoid major expenses by repairing the minor items before they become a bigger problem
- Happier tenant, who appreciates that you care about their well being
- Inspections recorded in case documentation is needed for insurance purposes
- Maintains value of the property
- Lower tenant turnover

Why do Background Checks on Tenants?

When I was young, a very smart person gave me the following words of wisdom:

"If you do not want chaos in your home, then do not allow it in the front door."

Screening tenants is an art when it comes to property management. The property manager should have the following company standards when it comes to screening tenants:

- Proof of stability of employment in their work history. Will the tenant be able to pay the rent each month? Many investors require 3x the rent as income in order for the applicant to qualify as a tenant. Property management should require copies of the last two pay stubs to verify tenant income.

- Look at credit history report (if the property manager pulls the credit — and they should — they cannot share the written document with anyone).
- Ask how many adults and children will be living at home to comply with city and state standards when it comes to occupancy laws.
- Ask for proof of identity to show the applicant is over 18.
- Run a background check that includes criminal record, evictions and credit score. The property manager should do a national background check by a private investigator.
- Verify rental history by calling the tenant's past landlord to confirm they are a good candidate to rent the property. The more information, the better to qualify a tenant when it comes to property management. Better yet, call the landlord before the current one, as the current landlord may be trying to pass off a less-than-desirable tenant.

Remember: You may be dealing with credit-challenged tenants — which is OK, as long as there is no evidence of felonies, evictions or too many past-due accounts.

Evictions are Part of Real Estate Investing

Evict (e vikt') – to recover property from a person by legal process. To put a tenant out by legal process.

Arizona (as an example) is a real estate investor-friendly state, compared to other states. An owner can remove a tenant by legal process in about 30 days from start to finish. That is good for an owner to know. This way the owner can turn the property to make rent-ready to place another qualified paying tenant to start generating money with collectable rent. Other states may drag out the eviction process for months, which means the tenant has stopped paying rent.

Let's Break Down the Arizona Eviction Process

- **5-Day Notice**: A notice indicating the amount due by tenant. This notice can be delivered either by hand or by certified mail. The tenant either cures this notice or will be sent to evictions.
- **Forcible Detainer is Filed**: Tenant's file includes forcible detainer with copies of

lease, ledger and five-day notice to be sent over to the lawyer's office.

- **Court Date**: Tenants have their day in court for failure to pay rent. The first question the judge will ask the tenant will be, "Did you pay your rent?" The tenant will have to answer either "Yes" or "No" per the judge. The judge will automatically grant judgment in favor of the owner for failure to pay rent. The judge will give the tenant five calendar days to pay what he or she owes. The owner has the following choices to make:

    » Accept the monies and allow the tenant to stay in property with a new lease

    » Accept the monies and remove the tenant from the property

    » Allow tenants to move out in five days and send tenant to collections

- **Writ of Restitution**: If the tenant fails to move out by the date granted by the court, then the owner has the right to file a writ of restitution. This is a court order from the judge to allow the local constable to remove the tenant from the property and to change locks to take back possession of the property.

- **Conduct Final Move-Out Inspection**: Property manager to conduct a final move-out inspection to determine a budget to make unit rent-ready. The security deposit is applied to monies owed plus any damages caused by the tenant. A security disposition letter is sent to the tenant to allow them to make good on the amount owed. Finally, tenant is sent to collections, which could lead to wage garnishment if necessary.

Remember that different states have very different eviction laws, so check with the municipality where your investment property is located.

Health and Safety Notices in Property Management

Real estate investing is very rewarding in the long run. The three phases in real estate investing can be summed up below:

1. Identify and purchase real estate
2. Rehab the property to make rent-ready
3. Place tenants, then develop a landlord-tenant relationship

Steps 1 and 2 may be the easiest. Now, the third step is enjoyable when there a good tenant. However, what does the investor do when there is a difficult tenant? Therefore, an investor needs a relationship with a professional property manager who knows how to deal with difficult situations for the real estate asset to keep moving forward.

The investor and property management need to know when and how to legally use the health and safety notices when it comes to property management. Tenants can live in the property if they pay rent and maintain the property per the lease agreement. Many single landlords fail to enforce the lease to protect their real estate investment. Then, the owner is spending more money when the tenant moves out when the lease ends.

Remember that if the tenant does damage to the property while the lease is in effect, the property management can repair the damage and bill the tenant immediately for the damage instead of waiting until the end of the lease and then deducting from the security deposit.

There are different kinds of notices that are used when it comes to property management:

10-Day Health and Safety Notices

The 10-day health and safety notices are utilized when you want the tenant to rectify a violation of the lease that needs attention. Examples of a 10-day violation would be: garbage that needs to be picked up from the yard, loud noise after hours, and not following HOA regulations. This would be considered a first offense and a warning to the tenant that an item needs to be addressed in 10 days. If it is not addressed, then it is possible to issue a second 10-day notice. The landlord will have the right to terminate the lease if the tenant continues to violate the lease for the same offense.

5-Day Health and Safety Notices

The 5-day notices pack a bigger punch. The tenant needs to satisfy the issue in five days, or the landlord will have the right to evict the tenant. The most famous 5-day notice is when the tenant does not pay rent. Also use the 5-day notice when it comes to hoarding, parking abandoned cars, unauthorized person or animal in the house and other serious infractions to ensure that the terms of the lease are enforced on behalf of the owner.

Immediate Notices

Immediate notices are given to tenants who commit a crime on the property that pertain to guns, drugs, violence, gangs and/or prostitution, to mention some of the serious things that can happen at a property. Immediate notices lead to immediate eviction in order to remove the problem. Then, the property manager will get the unit rent ready to place another paying tenant to keep the asset performing for the owner.

Chapter 8
PROPERTY INSPECTIONS

Home Inspections (1-4 Units)

A property inspector performs a very valuable and important service. A professional property inspector examines an existing home using professional standards as a measure to accurately report its condition to parties involved in the real estate transaction. The property inspector does not evaluate the property for cost or value, but reports objectively, in writing, the condition of the property's systems as they appear and operate at the time of the inspection.

A detailed property inspection will take as long as needed to evaluate the property's condition. Several factors will determine the length of time for the inspection, such as the property's age and square footage.

It is recommended that you be present at your property inspection so that you can ask your inspector any questions and look at any areas needing maintenance or repair.

The investor will be presented with a property inspection report, which will conform to the standards of practice for the State of Arizona. The inspection report will reflect those items that are visible or can be observed and reported on. The inspection report is not a home warranty. There may be items addressed in the inspection report as required by the state standards of practice that may not be relative to the negotiation process. Your commercial Broker will review the inspection report with you to formulate a response to the seller to address the findings in the inspection report. Any questions about the report should be addressed to the home inspector.

The State of Arizona requires that all home inspectors be registered with the Board of Technical Registration (BTR). To qualify to become a certified home inspector one must:

- Take specialized instruction from an approved school

- Pass the school test
- Pass the national test
- Complete 30 co-inspections with a certified home inspector
- Submit the reports from those co-inspections to the BTR for review to ensure conformity to the state requirements
- Carry the minimum requirements for insurance (Errors & Omissions – E&O – and Liability) or a bond in the amount prescribed by the BTR

Home inspectors are fully trained in the proper operation of all commonly found home systems. These systems generally include:

- Structural components: Foundation, floors and walls.
- Exterior components: Siding, paint, windows, decks, garage doors, etc.
- Roofing: Coverings, flashings, chimneys, etc.
- Plumbing: Piping, fixtures, faucets, water heating and fuel storage systems, etc.
- Electrical: Wiring, main service panels, conductors, switches, receptacles, etc.
- Heating: Equipment, safety controls, distribution systems, chimney, etc.
- Air conditioning and heat pumps: Cooling and air-handling equipment, controls and ducting, etc.
- Interior: Partitions, ceilings, floors, railings, doors and windows, etc.
- Insulations and ventilation: Attics, walls, floors, foundation, kitchen and bathrooms, etc.

When purchasing a property, many buyers have saved literally thousands of dollars through information provided by the property inspector.

If after evaluating the inspection results, the buyer decides to cancel the escrow, this is the best money that you can spend in order to not buy the "problem child" in the neighborhood. It's OK to find issues; the investor just needs to know what they are.

Commercial Inspections

Currently there is not a state requirement for inspections covering commercial properties including, but not limited to, multifamily structures, retail strip centers and office-warehouses. The scope for these inspections can be customized for the investor's particular needs and will be priced accordingly. The fundamental basis for the scope of work is to comment on the visible systems and deferred maintenance items observed. Any items that are covered or obscured from view cannot be commented on.

Multifamily dwellings (5+ units) including apartment buildings can be inspected with a scope of work similar to the standards used for 1- to 4-unit properties. The commercial narrative inspection report will include an estimate of costs to correct the items observed during the inspection. The estimated cost to cure is exactly that – an estimate. Your costs will vary. The inspection company should not offer construction services to correct items observed during the inspection process, as this could represent a conflict of interest.

The expectations for the commercial inspection report are more utilitarian in nature than for a home inspection. For example, in a home inspection, a comment of worn cabinets and countertops may warrant repairs, replacement or consideration from the seller. In a commercial inspection, a comment of worn cabinets and countertops may warrant a question whether or not the items are still serviceable with some maintenance or if the items can last for the expected time that the property will be held.

The inspection report, along with the direction of your commercial Broker, can provide a basis for negotiation of the property. The inspection process should be considered a tool in the purchasing process.

In addition to standard residential and commercial property inspections, additional inspections are occasionally required, including pool / spa, environmental (i.e., pre-1978 lead paint and asbestos testing), well, septic and termite. Your commercial Broker, with assistance from the property inspector, will help identify and arrange any additional services that a particular property may warrant. Fees for these additional inspections are typically extra but may be critical to understanding the condition of the property being purchased.

Entering Every Unit

The ASTM standard for property condition assessments (ASTM E2018) typically requires that 10% of a building be inspected. Often highly qualified inspectors specifically do not perform property condition assessments despite their official-sounding name and regular use by lenders. (They do have the training to perform property condition assessments, however).

In over 25 years of inspecting multifamily properties, and also large multi-tenant commercial/industrial properties, I have found that inspecting only 10% (or for that matter 20% or 30% of the units), can leave a buyer open to potentially significant unforeseen costs. Of course, inspecting 100% of the units can be a very expensive proposition, especially on larger apartment complexes and commercial properties.

A good commercial Broker and a good property inspector will know that a cost effective/

high value approach provides the buyer with lots of information about the property, while keeping inspection costs reasonable. The method for accomplishing this is by "detail" inspecting a low percentage of units based on the repetitive nature of most properties — typically 10%, but it can be higher or lower based on unique situations — and "overview" inspecting the balance of units.

Detail inspections are just that: very detailed. Overview inspections, in contrast, are relatively quick inspections focused on very specific high-cost defects including leaks, conditions conducive to mold formation, and electrical problems, primarily scorched subpanels. The inspector will also rate the overall cleanliness of the unit.

Using this approach, the time to capture the scope of routine issues, like missing GFCIs and smoke detectors, is during the detailed inspections which feed the final report. It also identifies the less routine, or frequent but typically more costly problems like roof leaks, water leaks, mold under the kitchen sink, and melted breakers.

Make sure that someone goes into EVERY unit, even the ones called storage rooms. The units that someone does not go into will be the worst. Do not take the word of the property manager or the seller. It is almost guaranteed that the unit that is not opened up will be the one that needs the most work.

It is strongly recommended that you use the "Entering Every Unit" approach on multifamily especially, but also with large, multi-tenant commercial properties.

Sewer Cameras

Property inspections typically exclude the buried portions of the sewer/drainage systems since the piping is not visible. The sewer systems at multifamily properties can be one of the biggest expenses if there are problems, since owners have little control over what tenants put in the sewer system. Even new apartment complexes can have problems. Having said that, and on commercial properties in general, it is strongly recommended that investors utilize a sewer camera on properties older than 1980 — or any age, if the property had a previous use as either a restaurant or medical facility.

So, what could go wrong with a sewer piping system? Root invasion is a common issue but easily dealt with if the piping system is in good condition and accessible. Deterioration of older type piping systems, including cast iron and orangeburg (named after the original factory in Orangeburg, N.Y.), can be expensive, especially if the piping is under the building or has other high-cost finished surface above the sewer line. Lining existing piping is a growing option but is only cost-effective in select situations.

A lack of cleanouts at ground level makes routine maintenance more difficult and costly.

Frequently older facilities don't have them, resulting in an initial cost to even gain access to the system for rootering or jetting.

Once the sewer cam report is received, it should be overlaid with any functional drainage issues observed during the inspection (many times the functional drainage test does not reveal blockages below, making the sewer cam all the more important).

Termite Inspections

The saying in some states is, "Every building either has termites, or is going to get them" — at least that is what termite treatment companies would like you to believe! While it is generally true, there are some old buildings in some areas that never seem to get termites and the theory is that they were treated with Chlordane many years ago. Possession of Chlordane is now a felony in the U.S., so that is no longer an option since it was killing the applicators as well as termites.

Dryer climates such as Arizona have two broad categories of termites. The vast majority is subterranean and easily treated with ground-applied chemicals. The newer chemicals, classified as termiticides, are particularly effective at killing the queen and hence, the colony, as opposed to less-expensive barrier chemicals that simply kill "incoming" worker termites.

The other type of termites is broadly classified as "airborne." These are much less common in the desert heat, but potentially trickier to treat. Even rarer are other classes of wood-destroying organisms (why this service is typically referred to as WDO) including the wood borers, which are specific beetles that literally bore through wood.

We highly recommend including termite (WDO) inspectors when completing an inspection since costs are relatively low.

Chapter 9
DOCUMENTATION

What Kind of Items Do You Need for Your Due Diligence?

While many investors ask for certain items for due diligence, many other items are overlooked. What should you be asking for?

First, some ground rules: No one can give you tenant credit reports. This is against federal law, so don't ask. Additionally, entities do not file Schedule E on their taxes, so don't ask. One item to note on the seller's tax returns: Most savvy investors write off as much as the law allows —and some even more so. So, the numbers that may be on the personal tax return (if the property is held in the seller's personal name) are irrelevant.

Something else that is often asked for are tenant estoppel certificates. For multifamily, all this request does is confuse the tenant, who often will actually leave the property, as the tenant does not understand what he or she is being asked. For a commercial building, estoppel certificates absolutely should be required. In fact, most commercial leases state the tenant will sign an estoppel certificate should the building be sold. This is a document either prepared by the buyer's attorney or escrow officer. It is simply an outline and the tenant's understanding of his or her lease.

Moving on to the meat of what is needed for the due diligence, some of the items on the following list may not be available, but be sure to ask anyway, or they may not be supplied even if the seller has them.

- Rent roll (showing tenant's name and terms of the lease along with any overdue balance)
- Full copies of the leases and all addendums
- Tenant applications (may not be supplied until Close of Escrow)

CHAPTER 9 — DOCUMENTATION

- Year-to-date financials
- Previous year's financials (called a "trailing 12")
- Previous year's rent roll by month
- Copies of any vendor contracts that will NOT expire at the Close of Escrow (laundry or vending machine leases, for example)
- Copies of any permits
- Copies of the commercial pool permit (if there is one)
- Copies of any warranties that convey
- Proof that all rental sales taxes have been paid
- A list of all capital improvements for the last two years along with receipts showing they have been paid for
- Seller's disclosure statements
- A 5-year insurance loss run
- Contact information for all service providers, along with the account numbers
- Certificate of Occupancy, if available
- Any outstanding litigation
- Any known pest infestation
- Schedule of personal property

Prior to close and if applicable, the seller will need to sign the documents and provide the passwords to websites, security systems and phone numbers that convey.

Remember that many owners will not have these items, and that's OK — to a degree. However, always get a signed written statement from the owner that he or she does not have the given item. This way, if it is found out later that the owner withheld information, the investor may have recourse against the seller.

At the least, do not settle for less than you feel is needed to get an accurate picture of how the property operates and is going to operate.

Do You Need to Install a Laundry Room?

Installing a laundry room in your multifamily property sounds like a great idea, but there are some factors to take into consideration.

As a landlord, your goal is to make money by attracting qualified, responsible tenants to the rental properties. Having a community laundry room is a great way to do that — especially if washers and dryers are not offered in individual units.

Attract Qualified Renters

A clean, well-maintained community laundry room in the residential building automatically makes the facility more attractive than the numerous rental properties that don't offer that necessary amenity. When people are looking at apartments, duplexes, and other rental properties, laundry is a top concern. The convenience of on-site laundry facilities is a huge selling point for potential renters who want to avoid the hassle of constantly going out to wash their clothes and planning their schedules according to the nearest laundromat's hours of operation. They can also avoid the financial and physical burden of purchasing and moving large washers and dryers to and from already cramped rentals that only provide washer and dryer hookups.

Create a Sense of Community

While socializing may not be the first thing that comes to mind when doing laundry, community laundry rooms can be a great place for residents to meet one another. Communal spaces in a residential building — like laundry rooms — provide a no-pressure, non-invasive space for tenants to get to know fellow residents and provide an immediate ice-breaker and conversation starter. Fostering a sense of community and providing spaces for your residents to connect can help to improve building safety and security, avoid major personal conflicts among tenants, and make your apartment complex a more neighborly and welcoming place to live overall.

Decrease Turnover

Every time a tenant moves out, the investor loses money. Not only is monthly income lost until there are new renters found, but the investor likely also will be paying to have the apartment professionally cleaned, advertise the vacancy, and make necessary upgrades in the unit. Every move also increases wear and tear on doorways, flooring, and walls, which can cost a lot in the long run. While it may not be the only reason a resident stays, a clean and well-kept community laundry room is definitely in the "pro" column. On the flip side, the inconvenience of not having proper laundry access on-site may cause renters to look elsewhere when it comes time to renew their lease.

Additional Income Opportunities

For many landlords, it comes down to the bottom line. While purchasing high-quality commercial laundry equipment and making the necessary plumbing and electricity adjustments may seem like a big investment, the additional revenue opportunities it provides can pay off in the long run.

Here are just a few of the ways that additional income from an on-site laundry room can be attained:

- Charge per wash and dry cycle
- Increase prices for wash upgrades and special features using state-of-the-art equipment
- Add dispensers for soap and other laundry products for residents to purchase
- Add additional vending machines in the laundry room, such as water or soda machines

In today's world, it's unwise for an investor to purchase coin-operated machines, as then someone has to collect the quarters, then hopefully all of the quarters make it to the bank. If the landlord chooses to purchase machines these days, be sure to purchase debit- or card-operated machines.

There are companies that will not only supply the machines but will maintain them, as well. This also goes for the additional vending machines.

Chapter 10
FOREIGN NATIONALS

Canadians Investing in the USA

Tips for Canadians

In addition to the Top 10 considerations list we have shared with you, we would like to cover the Canadian Investment Property Documentation and Financing Process. When you work with a commercial real estate Broker, you will have access to a network of funding relationships. Depending on the type of property, the background of the borrower and the plans for holding period and exit strategies, your commercial real estate Broker will recommend the best lender for you. In purchasing an investment property in the United States, prudently maximizing the financial leverage of property ownership, you will work with a mortgage broker who believes in two very important things:

- Completing your transaction calls for an open partnership including your loan representative, a support team that is effective and efficient in getting the right documentation to the lender for quicker approvals, and you, the borrower – who understands a successful loan cannot be possible without your being actively engaged in the process.

- Mortgage approvals are often considered complex and cumbersome, but with the right approach, they can be made easier.

There are some rather harsh realities with which we must deal in today's lending environment, and whether you are buying an investment home or refinancing an existing home loan, increasingly rigid guidelines make even well-qualified borrowers sometimes feel as if they are being made to jump through unnecessary hoops to qualify for their financing. Our job is to assist with gathering the essential documents that ensure you make the best possible first impression on the lender of choice – while meeting that lender's specific guidelines.

CHAPTER 10 — FOREIGN NATIONALS

As your partner in this process, the commercial Broker can only work as quickly as you are willing and able to provide the necessary documentation. Keep in mind that whether dealing with a processor, loan officer or mortgage broker – we do not make the rules or establish the guidelines – we simply step in as the facilitator to aid you in making the right choices and providing the correct documentation in the most efficient manner.

Documentation

In much the same way you wonder how to structure a resume to be considered for employment, loan submissions must be given the same serious supporting information. So that you are not offended when asked for certain items, understand that there are four key areas involved in the underwriting process:

1. The capacity of the borrower to pay interest and principal due on the loan, property taxes and homeowner's insurance, and all other current financial obligations.

2. The character of the borrower, based on the history reflected on the credit report and the indication of a solid asset base or history of owning investment properties. These provide the essential documentation of what the lender can realistically expect from the borrower's past behavior.

3. The amount of capital a borrower has for down payment and future reserves, or history of saving that gives the underwriter the assurance this loan will be a good risk.

4. The safety and soundness of the home and its coincident value determine the collateral the lender has, relative to the purchase price and the loan for which the lender is assuming future risk.

Loan Approval Guidelines

Although we spend extensive time in researching the lending sources that are most amenable to supporting the purchase of U.S. properties by persons who are not citizens of the United States, there is still a list of items we must have in hand before we can submit the loan for approval. Given the nature of the product that will be used to fund your purchase transactions, please use this checklist and provide the documents as quickly as possible. At the very minimum, virtually all lending products require the following:

Purchase: Primary Documentation Relative to the Borrower

- Signed copies of the prior past two years' tax returns and all attached "Schedules." If you are self-employed please add a signed and dated document reflecting the number of years you have been employed and the general nature of your profession.

- If your industry is licensed, provide a copy of that business license; if you own a partial interest in the company, provide a letter from your accountant confirming the percentage of ownership in your company, and how long you have owned it.

- Recent copy of a credit report for each borrower on the application. (Your Broker usually will obtain this.)
- One full month of paycheck stubs. Please make note of the frequency of payment, i.e. 1st and 15th, twice a month, once a month, annual salary, etc.
- Copies of your last two years' T4s.
- All pages of the past three months of all banking and/or asset/investment account statements. If the report is quarterly, provide the last two quarterly reports.
- Signed copies of the loan application and all associated "Disclosure" documents provided to you in process of your applying for a loan.
- Clear, enlarged copy of the driver's license for each borrower on the application.

Additional paperwork frequently required, if applicable to your particular situation:

- If you have filed for bankruptcy in the past 10 years, you will need to provide a copy of your final bankruptcy release.
- If you are receiving pension revenue, you may need to provide a copy of your award statement, reflecting the income that can be expected to continue for the next three years.
- If you own multiple properties, you will need to complete a Real Estate Owned Matrix.

Purchase: Primary Documents Relative to the Property

- Verification of clear title, preliminary title and escrow instructions, which will be managed on your behalf by the parties representing you in your investment purchase transaction.
- Information supporting coverage for homeowner's insurance. In most instances, this coverage will be facilitated on your behalf by the company you have elected to represent you in the purchase of your United States investment property.
- When you are applying for financing to purchase a home, please keep in mind that until your Broker receives a fully executed contract, escrow is opened and earnest money is received for a property, they cannot lock a rate or distribute fees/disclosures based on any particular scenarios.
- The contract is expected to be provided by the company representing you in your transaction.
- Verification of an established Limited Liability Company (LLC) or an LLLP in Arizona and copy of the underlying Operating Agreement (if applicable). This

document will be provided by the law firm responsible for assisting you with this process.

- Verification of the sourcing of your down payment (earnest money). Unless there is something unusual in the manner in which you will be providing your earnest money, the assumption will be made that you transferred funds from an existing account to the trust fund for the real estate company. Those funds were then transferred into a bank account in the name of your LLC or LLLP, ultimately utilized in your purchase transaction. If the money placed in the trust fund did not originate in an existing checking, savings or investment account, please clearly communicate the particulars so that your Broker can appropriately note that information to the Satisfactory Appraisal by the lender-approved appraisal services. You will be required to absorb the cost of this appraisal, and a copy will be provided upon receipt. The lender normally makes all the arrangements for managing this transaction item.

The Process

Some people become confused or feel misled by the lending terms such as mortgage approval, mortgage pre-approval, loan qualification and pre-qualification; each is an essential but separate part of the lending process.

- Pre-approvals ore pre-qualifications are just what they state – given the information provided, and all things being documentable – a green light to submit documents which verify the statements you made in your application to a lender for approval, based on that information meeting underwriting guidelines.

- The submitted file is carefully reviewed by a mortgage underwriter who again verifies the information and confirms nothing violates federal and/or lender-specific guidelines. It is not uncommon for an underwriter to ask for additional information either to justify something that is unclear or to strengthen the file by providing information that reduces the lender's risk. Once the underwriter is satisfied, you will receive an approval and clear to close. Then the actual closing is scheduled. It is important to make no significant changes in your income or asset base until your loan has fully closed.

Winning at the loan approval process means you have to play by the rules! Well-qualified buyers can inadvertently knock themselves out of the game if they make any substantive changes in their financial situation after the loan application has been submitted, but before the loan has closed. Keep in mind that the picture you painted for the lender at the time of application must be the same one the lender would see on the day of closing.

The following precautions apply:

1. Don't further dilute your asset base – hold off until your loan is complete before you

consider any major purchase.

2. Don't challenge the lender's request for ongoing documentation. It is not uncommon that the information noted in paperwork already provided prompts the need to meet yet another underwriting guideline that must be documented by additional papers. In an ever-changing lending environment, the best way to get through the process is to respond to requests as quickly as possible.

3. Work expediently through the process. Your rate has been established based on the market conditions at the time your application was taken; once locked, there is a limited time for which that lock is offered, and to prolong that process may jeopardize your right to that rate.

While everyone can certainly be empathetic that this appears to be a lot of information to have to assimilate in one sitting, it is a vital step in the process. This is why it's important to review this overview and a checklist where you can mark each document provided. Most conversations with your loan originator and following communications with a team member of the bank who may be processing the loan may feel overwhelming; all new experiences tend to provide that kind of feeling. This will also serve as a letter of encouragement, that checklist of items and information you will need to provide, and a guideline of what is expected and how you can best plan to win in the approval process.

Other Nationals Investing in the USA
Tips for Australians Investing in U.S. Property

Background

Like all non-resident investors in U.S. real property, Australians need to be aware of rules in three different areas: U.S. tax law, Australian tax law and the U.S.-Australian tax treaty. The rules and procedures from a U.S. perspective are similar to any other country with which the U.S. has an income and capital tax treaty.

Investors are going to have to file U.S. tax returns every year (1040NR), obtain a U.S. tax identification number (ITIN), FIRPTA, and be aware of U.S. estate tax, etc.

U.S. Tax

As with Canadians, Australian residents are afforded opportunities for U.S. estate tax exemptions, annual foreign tax credits, deductions to income, etc. This also means that only U.S. domiciled property is subject to estate tax, and they are entitled to a prorated exemption of the U.S. estate tax.

Taxes will be paid on income earned in the U.S. first to the IRS, and foreign tax credits will be given when they file their personal income tax returns in Australia.

Australian Tax

Australia has a higher marginal tax rate on ordinary income (rental income) than the U.S., with a top marginal rate of 45%, a 1.5% Medicare tax on taxable income and a maximum 1% flood levy tax. Like the U.S., Australia taxes partnership income in the hands of the partners and not at the partnership level. The corporate rate is a flat 30% of income. Australian trusts, with some exceptions, are taxed at the rate of ultimate beneficiaries.

Capital gains are taxed at the taxpayer's marginal tax rate. However, if the asset is held for more than one year, then the taxpayer receives a 50% reduction in the capital tax treatment; if holding the assets for less than 12 months, the taxpayer gets a lower tax rate.

One important thing to know about Australia is that minors who receive income are taxed at the top marginal rate after only a couple thousand dollars of income, so income-splitting with kids is not tax-efficient.

Business Structure

In 2003, the Australian treasury department took a different stance from that of Canada on "hybrid companies" that were formed overseas. Before that date, U.S. LLCs and LLLPs were treated as "corporations" and thus subject to a tax inside the company and another tax when the income was distributed to the partners or members. When Australia took its revised position on the tax treatment of these U.S. hybrid companies, it made it possible for Australians to own U.S. LLCs directly without double tax issues back home in Australia. The rules say that in order for the LLC to be considered a flow-through in Australia, it has to be a flow-through in the U.S. These new rules do not include U.S. trusts or grantor trusts.

Conclusion

It is possible from an Australian standpoint to own U.S. real property through a single-member LLC as a shield from liability exposure. However, when two or more partners are investing, it makes sense from a cost perspective to have a parent LLLP or LLC and then hold the properties in a single-member LLC to create a liability protection for each of the properties.

Chapter 11
TAXES AND THE IMPLICATIONS

Tax Benefits of a Business in Real Estate

If you decide to invest in real estate, particularly for residential or commercial rental use, you have essentially gone into business, and there are many tax benefits to owning such a business.

It is important to consider all of the possible forms of ownership and the tax benefits of each. You can own a business as any of the following:

- Sole Proprietorship
- Partnership
- Limited Liability Company (LLC)
- C-Corporation
- S-Corporation

Your Certified Public Accountant (CPA), in partnership with a good attorney, can properly guide you in forming the entity that is right for you, by considering your own individual needs, goals and circumstances.

Tax Planning

When you're ready to invest, your CPA will want to meet with you to project possible scenarios of your investment. You will need to know how different investment avenues and the timing of such investments can affect your investment decision. The tax laws are constantly changing. The United States Congress acts on tax matters several times every year, and you can expect that your CPA is keeping up with the ever-changing tax laws.

A recent major tax change is the Tax Cuts and Jobs Act of 2017. Most of the provisions of the Act went into effect for the 2018 tax year. The effects are far-reaching and will continue to evolve over the next few years. Already there have been numerous regulations and notices put out by the IRS to provide for greater clarity and direction. The TCJA contains numerous provisions affecting investors and businesses, such as the Qualified Business Income Deduction and 100-percent bonus depreciation on certain qualifying property.

Keeping Your Books

One of the most critical aspects of operating your business is keeping good accounting records. Whether your CPA does most of this for you, or you have someone qualified to do the basic day-to-day bookkeeping in-house, this is an area of your business that should never be neglected. If you do get behind, however, rest assured that your CPA will be able to help you reorganize and bring your records up to date.

Your CPA can help you select appropriate bookkeeping software, or a more simplified manual system that will best meet your needs, while assuring that you are producing records that will assist your CPA in meeting your more complex accounting and tax compliance requirements.

Interim and Annual Reporting

Your CPA should be able to produce, or assist you in producing, your own financial statements. A properly prepared financial statement should give you an accurate picture of the current financial state of your business and reflect a historical presentation of the income, expenses and profit or loss of your business for the period reported, whether monthly, quarterly, or annually. The CPA can also prepare forecasted financial statements to help you in planning.

A properly prepared financial statement can be an extremely useful tool in helping you manage your business and its investments. Your CPA should be able to assist you in understanding your financial statements, so that you can get the most out of the information presented.

Tax Compliance

Anyone in business has income tax reporting requirements. Some businesses also have sales tax (transaction privilege tax) and employment tax requirements. The tax laws are continually changing, and your CPA should have current expertise in each of these areas of tax law. The CPA will prepare all of the appropriate reports to keep you in compliance with the various government agencies, including the Internal Revenue Service and each required state and local agency.

Depreciation

When you purchase an asset that has a useful life that spans an extended period of time, you typically must expense it over that useful life. This is referred to as "depreciation." The IRS has assigned most assets to a specific depreciable life. The chart on the following page provides some examples of assets you may own as a real estate investor and the depreciation life assigned to each.

A safe harbor election for small taxpayers is available allowing improvements to be directly expensed when a series of conditions are present. Your CPA can advise as to whether your improvements qualify, and whether this election is to your benefit.

**A de minimis safe harbor election is available for amounts paid to acquire or produce tangible property up to $2500 per invoice or item ($5000 if you have an applicable financial statement). If a safe harbor election is made, such otherwise capitalized items can be directly expensed.*

Bonus Depreciation

From time to time, Congress passes legislation that allows for business assets to receive extra depreciation in the year of purchase. This bonus depreciation in the first year has sometimes been as much as 100% of the cost of the asset. Your CPA will know if you are eligible for bonus depreciation.

First Year Expensing (Section 179 Depreciation)

This special election allows you to depreciate all of the cost of certain assets in the year of purchase. For tax years 2018 and 2019, the aggregate cost of depreciable property a taxpayer can elect to expense under Code Section 179 cannot exceed $1,000,000. The limit is reduced on a dollar-for-dollar basis to the extent the total cost of eligible property placed in service during the year by the taxpayer exceeds $2,500,000. As a result of the new Tax Act, used equipment also qualifies for this benefit.

Travel Expenses

Let's suppose you live in Seattle or Vancouver, but own rental property in Phoenix, Arizona. You can take a tax deduction against your rental income for your cost to travel to and from Phoenix to check on your property, take care of business, or to meet with your attorney or CPA. This includes air travel, auto travel and lodging. For 2019, auto travel can be deducted at the standard mileage rate of 58 cents per mile. Any side trips you take, such as driving to Tucson to visit a relative, are not deductible, nor is an extra day's lodging to do shopping or attend a hockey game.

Financing Costs

Mortgage and bridge loan interest is a deductible expense. Various other loan fees and

DEPRECIATION LIFE OF ASSETS

Residential Real Property (excluding land value) ....27.5 years

Non-Residential Real Property (excluding land value) ....39 years

Most Residential Real Property Improvements* ....27.5 years

Most Non-residential Real Property Improvements* ....39 years

Qualified Improvement Property (Non-Residential) (Absent Technical Correction) .39 years

Land Improvements (Sidewalks, Parking Lots, Playground Equipment, etc) ....15 years

Trees or Vines Bearing Fruit or Nuts ....10 years

Office Furniture & Equipment..7 years

Office Computers ....5 years

Assets Used in Construction by Certain Contractors,
    Builders, and Real Estate Subdividers and Developers ....5 years

Assets Found in a Rental Property (Personal Property)**:

    Furniture..5 years

    Stove & Range Hood ....5 years

    Oven ....5 years

    Dishwasher ....5 years

    Refrigerator ....5 years

    Microwave Oven ....5 years

    Space Heaters ....5 years

    Window Air Conditioning Units...5 years

    Window Treatments ....5 years

    Carpeting ....5 years

origination fees (points) are amortized and deducted over the life of the loan. If you pay off the loan early, any remaining unamortized cost is deductible in the year of payoff.

Not all legitimate business expenses are tax deductible. Here are a couple of examples of Nondeductible Business Expenses requiring separate reporting:

- Penalties
- Entertainment
- Business meals (only 50% is deductible)

There are many other possible deductions you can take against your rental income, and your CPA is available to guide you in getting the greatest tax benefit allowable.

The Tax Cuts and Jobs Act of 2017– Highlights

The Tax Cuts and Jobs Act of 2017 is the boldest piece of tax legislation since The Tax Reform Act of 1986. While the TCJA was billed as tax simplification, it is anything but simple. Both individuals and businesses should be aware of the major changes. Here are a few of the highlights affecting individuals:

- Personal exemptions eliminated
- Individual tax rates generally reduced
- State and local combined tax deduction limited to $10,000
- Employee business expense deduction eliminated
- Standard deduction in lieu of itemized deduction increased to $12,000 if Single, $24,000 if Married Filing Jointly and $18,000 if Head of Household
- Child tax credit increased

Some of the most complex changes affect businesses and investors. Some highlights include the following:

Corporate Income Tax Rate

The maximum corporate income tax rate is now 21%. This rate applies to corporations taxed at the corporate level (C-Corporations). In some cases, this form of entity structure is now more desirable as a result of the decrease in tax rate. However, one should be mindful that double-taxation is still a consideration and should be weighed against the reduced rate. Oftentimes, the C-Corporation structure is most desirable when the business intends to use profits to invest in significant income-producing capital. International taxpayers should compare the tax laws in their resident country when making this choice.

Qualified Business Income Deduction

The TCJA added a new deduction for pass-through and sole proprietorship income, in order to provide some relief to non-corporate taxpayers. The QBI deduction is taken at a rate of 20% of net income from partnerships, S-Corporations and sole proprietors.

There are some exclusions for specified service industries at certain income levels. There is also an exclusion for the casual rental property investor. Although information regarding QBI is provided by the partnership or S-Corporation in the case of a pass-through entity, the QBI deduction is taken on the taxpayer's individual tax return.

Safe Harbor for Rental Real Estate

Due to considerable question as to whether the IRS would consider the rental of real property as a business for purposes of taking the QBI deduction, the IRS issued regulations in January 2019, which provided a safe harbor for rental real estate to be treated as a trade or business. Here are some key takeaways from the new provision:

- 250 hours or more per year of rental services are performed with respect to the business.

- Triple net leases are specifically prohibited from using the safe harbor. They must be analyzed outside the safe harbor to determine eligibility for the deduction.

- Separate books and records must be maintained for each enterprise.

- The taxpayer must maintain contemporaneous records, including time reports, logs or similar documents regarding hours of all services performed, a description of all services performed, dates on which the services were performed and who performs the services.

- The rental services can be performed by owners, employees, agents or independent contractors.

- Qualifying rental services do not include financial or investment management activities.

- Taxpayers have the option to aggregate multiple rental businesses when calculating the 250 hours.

Not being eligible to use the safe harbor does not automatically preclude the QBI deduction. Each business will have its own set of qualifying factors. And keep in mind that safe harbor is just that — a safe harbor. Your CPA can help you determine if you are eligible for this deduction.

Business Interest Expense Deduction Limitation

Some important changes have been made with respect to deductibility of business interest expense that exceeds 30% of adjusted taxable income. However, there is an exemption from this limitation in most cases, when a prior three-year average of gross receipts does not exceed $25 million. Real estate businesses are eligible to make a one-time irrevocable election to not be subject to the limitation. However, if the election is made, there is a lost benefit regarding certain favorable depreciation methods. Your CPA can help you determine if the election would work to your benefit.

Chapter 12
HOW DO YOU PAY FOR THE PROPERTY?

Single-Family to Fourplex Investment Financing

Buying a single-family house, duplex, triplex, or fourplex can be a good investment for both investors and residential home buyers. Purchasing small multi-unit properties requires some basic understanding of how to locate, finance, and manage multiple units. Those activities are only slightly more involved than buying single-family properties but can lead to a profitable multi-unit investment.

The good news is that unlike a commercial loan, the 1- to 4-unit tenant-occupied loan is 25% down and amortized over 30 years at a fixed rate.

The investor will need to take title in his or her own name and provide all of the same documentation as when qualifying for a personal residence.

The lender will take into consideration 75% of the actual income on the property, if it is occupied, as income to the borrower.

The length of the escrow is typically 30-45 days, and it is handled much the same as the residential purchase of personal real estate. The main difference is that copies of the leases and a current rent roll must be provided to the title company and the lender.

Additionally, the investor can actually buy as an owner-occupied using a conventional, FHA or VA loan. It is critical to note that when using owner-occupied financing, the OWNER must live in the property — no exceptions. The loan limits are much higher for VA and FHA for 2-3-4 units. Also important to note is that within 60 days from the close of escrow, the unit that will be occupied must be vacant and the owner/investor must move into the unit.

Typically, with the purchase of an owner-occupied 2-3-4, the Broker will need to find month-to-month leases that are in place. Please be aware that few sellers will notice a tenant to move until the buyer has removed all contingencies.

Multifamily and Commercial Investment Financing

Financing strategies for a multifamily residential investment property are distinctly different than those that might be considered when buying a new home. The investor must first consider the hold period.

How long do the investors intend to hold the property? Given the ups and downs of market trends, it is a good idea to review the investor financial position with any property every two to three years. Therefore, the investor should be selecting a loan for the benefit of the first two or three years. If the investor position is still strong, it may be a good time to refinance the property after three years. The investor will have the option to capture and leverage the appreciation or secure a longer-term loan at a lower loan-to-value.

Second, multifamily residential loans are on the higher end of the lender's pricing model due to the risk involved with recovering a property in default. Here are some things to keep in mind when evaluating the investor options:

Be aware that any fixed-rate loan will be substantially higher than the investor will see on a primary residence. Unless the investor chooses to pay a discount point to buy down the rate, it is better to stay with a shorter-term ARM loan, which will have a lower rate, creating greater cash flow.

Cash flow is king when it comes to selecting a loan for a couple reasons.

The more down payment the investor can make, the lower the interest rate and the greater the cash flow.

The second reason is that when buying a new multifamily property, there can be turnover in tenants in the first few months of ownership. If the investor loan has a low minimum monthly payment, the investor can handle the vacancies that may occur from time to time without having to dig into his or her own pocket to make a payment. If the investor experiences low vacancies, take the monthly income and re-invest it! the investor profits then become exponential.

The investor interest rate is usually based on the following index:

- Monthly Treasury Average (12 MTA): The 12 MTA index is based on yields published in the release entitled the "Selected Interest Rates H-15," which is published by the Federal Reserve Board on the first Tuesday of each month. The investor performs a simple calculation of averaging the preceding 12-month annual yield to come up with the current index value that is published on the pricing guide.

Why and How do Interest Rates Change?

Many people are surprised to learn that rates change on a daily and sometimes hourly basis. Interest rates fluctuate in response to changes in the financial markets. The bond market is generally a good indicator of the general trend of interest rates.

What is Mortgage Insurance?

This is generally required in one form or another when the down payment is less than 20% and protects the lender in the event of loan default. The lower the down payment on the property, the higher the risk for the lender; therefore, the higher the monthly premium. Depending on the investor particulars, there are ways in which mortgage insurance can sometimes be avoided at purchase, or dropped altogether at some point in the future.

Multifamily / Commercial Pre-Qualification Checklist

The following items will be needed in order to pre-qualify a deal:

- A personal financial statement dated within the last 60 days.
- A tri-merge credit report dated within 60 days. (Lender will pull.)
- The last two years' and year-to-date income operating expense statement for the property.
- If more than one unit, a copy of the rent roll dated within the last 60 days.
- A copy of the purchase contract and earnest money check, if applicable.
- A brief summary of the loan requested, which should include who, what, where, when, why and how. (Lender will complete.)
- A resume from the borrower showing landlord / investment experience.
- Digital color photos of the property. (Inspector to provide.)

Worried About Credit?

Are there any worries about the investor credit history? Just about everyone has something in their past credit that is less than perfect. The most important thing is to learn what is on the investor report, determine what impact that information has on the investor credit rating, and work on repairing any damage that may have been done so the investor can restore the investor good credit standing.

Mortgage loan options are rated by credit, labeled like school grades: "A" credit is the best, then down to A-, B, C, etc. Even if the investor does not have an A credit rating, the Broker can let the investor know what the investor options are if the investor falls into an A- or lower category. The rates are generally going to be higher and may require a larger down payment. If the investor is not satisfied with this type of financing, then he or she and the Broker can map out what the investor needs to do with his or her credit and finances for the next six to 12 months in order to qualify for a credit loan.

There are three main credit bureaus to which most creditors (such as credit card companies, banks, leasing companies, etc.) provide information. Each month, the investor credit holders report information to the credit bureaus about the investor current balance, minimum payment requirements and credit history. If the investor needs specific information from one of the major credit bureaus, following is the contact information for each:

Experian Information Service (XPN)
P.O. Box 2002
Allen, TX 75013
(888) 397-3742
www.experian.com

TransUnion (TUC)
P.O. Box 1000
Chester, PA 79022
(800) 916-8800
www.transunion.com

Equifax Information Services (EFX)
P.O. Box 740243
Atlanta, GA 30374
(800) 685-1111
www.equifax.com

Why are Higher Scores Good? It's all About the Likelihood of Default

The investor might be wondering why lenders feel so compelled to charge someone more for a lower FICO score. Let's take a look at FICO scores from the perspective of the investor who is going to personally lend someone some money. If I were to ask the investor to borrow $5,000, the investor would want to know whether I was a pretty good bet to repay the investor, right? Of course, the investor would.

In looking at the chart, the investor can see that if my FICO score was over 800, Fair

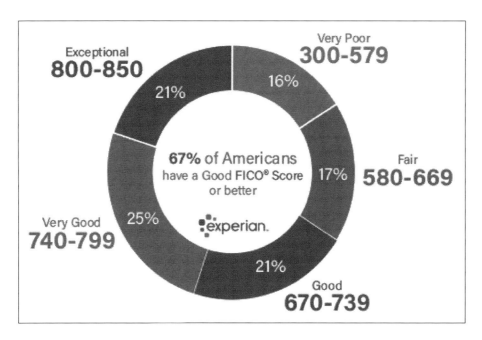

Isaac and Company, the Las Vegas of the credit world, will tell the investor that the investor can be 99% sure that I will pay the investor back or as illustrated here for the investor, there is a 1% chance I'm going to default on my loan with the investor. If my score falls into the range of, say, 550-559, the investor might see the investor money and the investor might not. The scores will tell the investor that I only have a 49% chance of repaying the investor. And finally, if my scores are below 500, forget it. The investor only stands a 17% chance of getting repaid. So, as the scores fall, it's easy to see why someone would want to charge a higher rate of interest.

Credit Score Factors

Now that we know the price someone could pay by having a low score, it's important to have a better understanding of how these scores are calculated so borrowers can work to keep theirs as high as possible.

In essence, there are five general components of a FICO score. One thing to remember, it's not just whether the investor pays his or her bills on time. In fact, we have seen cases where someone has never had a late payment and had scores in the high 500s. As we see here, the results from having a clean payment history just wouldn't serve the investor well enough.

Payment history is merely 35% of the score. The amount owed, or the way the credit is handled, accounts for another 30%. The length of time cards or other credit accounts have been opened comprises another 15% and new credit and the types of credit used account for another 10% each.

The Five Factors of Credit Scoring

1. PAYMENT HISTORY: 35%

- A recent 30-date-late can cost 50+ points.
- Paying a collection that is more than two years old can hurt a score.
- Being past due on an account can cost 50+ points.
- Derogatory accounts do NOT always fall off of a credit report automatically after seven years; they must be disputed.
- A divorce decree does NOT take precedence over the creditor agreement.

2. AMOUNTS OWED: 35%

- New debt temporarily decreases a score.
- Balances should be kept below 50% at all times to maintain a score.
- Balances should be kept below 30% of the limit for three to six months prior to applying for a home loan.
- Debt should NOT be consolidated; it should be distributed evenly over all credit card accounts.
- Going over the limit on a credit card, even by $1, will cause a serious penalty.
- HELOCs can be considered revolving debt, not mortgages.
- Credit card accounts should NOT be closed except in special circumstances.
- Unused credit card accounts will become unrated in three months.

3. LENGTH OF HISTORY: 15%

- Borrowers should hold onto old credit cards, even if the rate is not great.
- New credit users can NO LONGER add themselves to another person's account as an authorized user to generate a score.

4. MIX OF CREDIT: 10%

- Mixture is the best.
- The type of credit card DOES matter.
- Three to five revolving credit cards with established history is optimal.

5. INQUIRES: 10%

- Hard vs. soft inquiries.
- 14-day window for pulling reports.

- Inquiries affect a score for one year.
- Inquiries can cost between 2 and 30 points, depending on the current score.
- Pre-approved card offers are NOT really pre-approved.

Differences Between Bridge and Mezzanine Financing

A bridge loan is a short-term loan that "bridges" the borrower's plan from point A to point B. The borrower only needs financing for a very short time frame, so a long-term fixed rate loan is not the solution. For example, a borrower may currently be in the process of selling his or her office building so that he or she can purchase a multifamily building; however, the money from the sale of the office building has not come through yet, and he or she needs to close on the second property. Therefore, the borrower needs a bridge loan to buy the second property, and then when the sale of the first property happens he or she can pay down the bridge loan.

A mezzanine loan can be a type of bridge loan in the same sense that it is short-term and not permanent financing. However, a mezzanine loan is not secured by property, but rather by an ownership interest in the company that owns the property. This occurs when the borrower needs more money than he or she is able to borrow against the property, so he or she puts up an interest in his or her company as collateral.

Bridge Financing

A bridge loan is collateralized by a senior lien on the underlying real estate asset. Loans usually range from $1 million to $10 million with terms from 30 days to three years. Each loan is unique in that it can include interest coupons structured as current pay or accrual and amortization schedules ranging from interest-only to fully amortizing. This type of financing can be utilized by owner/operators of real estate (i) to complete new acquisitions or developments; (ii) to recapitalize existing assets; (iii) to repurchase existing debt from current lenders; (iv) to acquire existing performing/non-performing mortgages; (v) to fund plans of reorganization or debtor-in-possession loans in the context of bankruptcy filings; or (vi) for other unique financing situations.

- Financing amount: $1 million to $10 million
- Pricing: 8% - 14%, usually
- Fees: 1-4 points, usually
- Term: Up to three years

- Amortization: Interest-only or amortizing
- Security: First Mortgage Lien
- LTC: Up to 80% (sponsor and asset specific) (LTC=Loan to Collateral)
- LTV: Up to 70% (sponsor and asset specific)
- Asset Class: All types of commercial real estate

Mezzanine Financing

There are companies that will provide mezzanine financing collateralized by either a direct lien on the underlying real estate or a lien on the ownership interest in real estate. Loans usually range from $1 million to $10 million with terms from one to three years. Each loan is unique in that it can include interest coupons structured as current pay or accrual and amortization schedules ranging from interest-only to fully amortizing. Financing can be utilized by owner/operators of real estate (i) to complete new acquisitions or developments; (ii) to recapitalize existing assets; (iii) to repurchase existing debt from current lenders; or (IV) to acquire existing performing/nonperforming mortgages.

- Financing amount: $1 million to $10 million
- Pricing: Rates and fees adjusted for risk and leverage
- Term: Up to three years
- Amortization: Typically not required
- Security: 100% pledge of ownership interest and/or second lien
- LTC: Up to 80%
- Uses: Acquisition, Recapitalization, Construction, Refinancing

Chapter 13
FORMULAS

What is the Capitalization Rate? (Cap Rate)

Cap Rate is the ratio between the Net Operating Income (NOI) produced by an asset and its cost. It is also an indirect way to determine how quickly the investment will pay for itself.

Remember that this does not include debt service. Another way to view the cap rate is that it is simply a picture of an asset's performance at a given point in time.

An investment at an 8% cap rate will pay for itself in 12.5 years. An investment with a cap rate of 10% will pay for itself in 10 years, etc. Below is an example of the cap rate, using the single-family example and its relation to purchase price.

A rule of thumb is that the higher the cap rate, the lower the price and vice versa.

CAP RATE		
8%	10%	12%
$75,000	$60,000	$50,000
$87,500	$70,000	$58,333
$100,000	$80,000	$65,000
$112,500	$90,000	$75,000
$125,000	$100,000	$83,333

What is the Loan-to-Value (LTV) Ratio?

The loan-to-value (LTV) ratio is a lending risk assessment ratio that financial institutions and other lenders examine before approving a mortgage. Typically, assessments with high LTV ratios are generally seen as higher risk and, therefore, if the mortgage is accepted, the loan will generally cost the borrower more or he or she will need to purchase mortgage insurance.

Calculated as:

$$\text{Loan to Value Ratio} = \frac{\text{Mortgage Amount}}{\text{Appraised Value of the Property}}$$

Breaking Down LTV Ratio

For example, let's say Jim needs to borrow $92,500 to purchase a $100,000 property. The LTV ratio yields a value of about 92.5%. Since bankers usually require a ratio at a maximum of 75% for a mortgage to be approved, it may prove difficult for Jim to get a mortgage.

Similar to other lending risk assessment ratios, the LTV ratio is not comprehensive enough to be used as the only criteria in assessing mortgages.

Breaking Down Debt-Service Coverage (DSCR) Ratio

A DSCR of less than 1 means negative cash flow. A DSCR of .95 means that there is only enough net operating income to cover 95% of annual debt payments. For example, in the context of personal finance, this would mean that the borrower would have to delve into his or her personal funds every month to keep the project afloat. In general, lenders frown on a negative cash flow, but some allow it if the borrower has strong outside income.

Net operating income is a company's revenue minus its operating expenses, not including taxes and interest payments. It is often considered equivalent to earnings before interest and tax (EBIT). Some calculations include non-operating income in EBIT, however, which is never the case for net operating income.

As a lender or investor comparing different companies' credit-worthiness — or a manager comparing different years or quarters — it is important to apply consistent criteria when calculating DSCR. As a borrower, it is important to realize that lenders may calculate DSCR in slightly different ways.

Total debt service refers to current debt obligations, meaning any interest, principal, sinking-fund and lease payments that are due in the coming year. On a balance sheet, this will include short-term debt and the current portion of long-term debt.

Income taxes complicate DSCR calculations, because interest payments are tax-deductible, while principal repayments are not. Therefore, a more accurate way to calculate total debt service is this:

$$DSCR = \frac{\text{Net Operating Income}}{\text{Total Debt Service}}$$

Net Present Value (NPV)

Net Present Value (NPV) is perhaps the most widely used of the three common rates of return. It represents the net present value of a series of cash flows, discounted at the cost of capital. NPV indicates how much value an investment adds to the company. If NPV > 0, then the investment may be accepted. If NPV <0, then the investment should be rejected. Below is an example of a single-family home investment; the cost of capital is 8%.

YEAR	CASH FLOW	PRESENT VALUE
Initial Investment Year 0	($80,000)	($80,000)
Year 1	$6,000	$5,556
Year 2	$7,000	$6,001
Year 3	$8,000	$6,351
Year 4	$9,000	$6,615
Year 5	$10,000	$6,806
Sale at end of Year 5	$125,000	$85,073
NPV		$36,402
IRR		17.54%

Cash-on-Cash Return

Cash-on-Cash Return is the annual net operating income divided by the net investment made. It is used as a quick way to compare return ratios to other investments, such as bank CDs. It works for investments that have consistent annual cash flows. It does not take into account price appreciation like the internal rate of return (IRR).

Cash-on-Cash Return
Each year of the 5-year hold, as illustrated previously in the Net Present Value
7.50%
8.75%
10.00%
11.25%
12.50%

What is the Internal Rate of Return?

When calculating the Internal Rate of Return (IRR), expected cash flows for a project or investment are given and the NPV equals zero. Put another way, the initial cash investment for the beginning period will be equal to the present value of future cash flows of that investment.

(Cost paid = present value of future cash flows, and hence, the net present value = 0).

Once the internal rate of return is determined, it is typically compared to a company's hurdle rate or cost of capital. If the IRR is greater than or equal to the cost of capital, the company would accept the project as a good investment. (That is, of course, assuming this is the sole basis for the decision. In reality, there are many other quantitative and qualitative factors that are considered in an investment decision.) If the IRR is lower than the hurdle rate, then it would be rejected.

CHAPTER 13 — FORMULAS

What is the IRR Formula?

The IRR formula is as follows:

$$0 = CF_0 + \frac{CF_1}{(1 + IRR)} + \frac{CF_2}{(1 + IRR)^2} + \frac{CF_3}{(1 + IRR)^3} + \ldots + \frac{CF_n}{(1 + IRR)^n}$$

OR

$$0 = NPV = \sum_{n=0}^{N} \frac{CF_n}{(1 + IRR)^n}$$

Where:

CF_0 = Initial Investment/Outlay

CF_1, CF_2, CF_3 ... CF_n = Cash flows

n = Each period

N = Holding period

Calculating the internal rate of return can be done in three ways:

1. Using the IRR or XIRR function in Excel or other spreadsheet programs
2. Using a financial calculator
3. Using an iterative process where the analyst tries different discount rates until the NPV equals zero (Goal Seek in Excel can be used to do this)

An example of how to calculate the Internal Rate of Return is shown on the following page.

YEAR	CASH FLOWS	PV OF CASH FLOWS
0	($500,000)	($500,000)
1	$160,000	$141,247
2	$160,000	$124,692
3	$160,000	$110,077
4	$160,000	$97,176
5	$50,000	$26,808

NPV	0
IRR	13%

A company is deciding whether to purchase new equipment that costs $500,000. Management estimates the life of the new asset to be four years and expects it to generate an additional $160,000 of annual profits. In the fifth year, the company plans to sell the equipment for its salvage value of $50,000.

Meanwhile, another similar investment option can generate a 10% return. This is higher than the company's current hurdle rate of 8%. The goal is to make sure the company is making better use of its cash.

What is Internal Rate of Return Used For?

Companies take on various projects to increase their revenues or cut down costs. A great new business idea may require, for example, investing in the development of a new product.

In capital budgeting, senior leaders like to know the reasonably projected returns on such investments. The internal rate of return is one method that allows them to compare and rank projects based on their projected yield. The investment with the highest internal rate of return is usually preferred.

Internal rate of return is widely used in analyzing investments for private equity and venture capital, which involves multiple cash investments over the life of a business and a cash flow at the end through an IPO or sale of the business.

Thorough investment analysis requires a commercial Broker (preferably a CCIM) to examine both the net present value (NPV) and the internal rate of return, along with other indicators, such as the payback period, in order to select the right investment. Since it's possible for a very small investment to have a very high rate of return, investors and managers sometimes choose a lower percentage return but higher absolute dollar value opportunity. Also, it's important to have a good understanding of the investor's own risk tolerance, or a company's investment needs, risk aversion, and other available options.

Chapter 14

HOW TO USE AND UNDERSTAND SPREADSHEETS

There are so many spreadsheets on the market for investors that it can be overwhelming. The following spreadsheets are for CCIM Commercial Brokers. Not only do these cover income both before- and after-taxes but also cap rates and internal rates of return before and after taxes.

It is important that the commercial Broker and the investor use the same spreadsheet. This way both parties are comparing apples to apples instead of apples to oranges. Ultimately, most spreadsheets are OK, but the more in-depth that the information is, the more sophisticated the spreadsheet will need to be.

What is good about using the following spreadsheets is that any property in the U.S. and any asset class that is income-producing can be put side by side for evaluation.

No matter which spreadsheet you use, be sure it answers the necessary questions to help you reach the right conclusion about the property under consideration.

This disclaimer applies to all the example spreadsheets that follow.

LICENSE

This file was developed for the CCIM Institute, which holds copyright to the CCIM Business Forms Templates. The authority granted to you to use this file and the Templates included permit use only in the regular course of doing business, including giving copies of reports generated by the Templates to clients, their agents and consultants. Your authority to use the Templates expressly excludes any right to sell, rent or otherwise use the Templates

CHAPTER 14 — HOW TO USE AND UNDERSTAND SPREADSHEETS

for the purpose of deriving a source of income.

These CCIM Business Forms Templates are made available for use on an "as-is" basis. Use of the Templates constitutes the user's waiver of any and all claims against the Institute and the author that may arise as a result of such use, including without limitation reliance on any conclusion indicated by the Template or any report generated by the Template, even if the Template is defective. All warranties, express or implied, are hereby disclaimed, including but not limited to any regarding the suitability of the Template for any application."

DCF Analysis V 11.5

© Copyright 2015 by the CCIM Institute. All rights reserved.

Example spreadsheets begin on the following page.

Investment Analysis — Single-Family

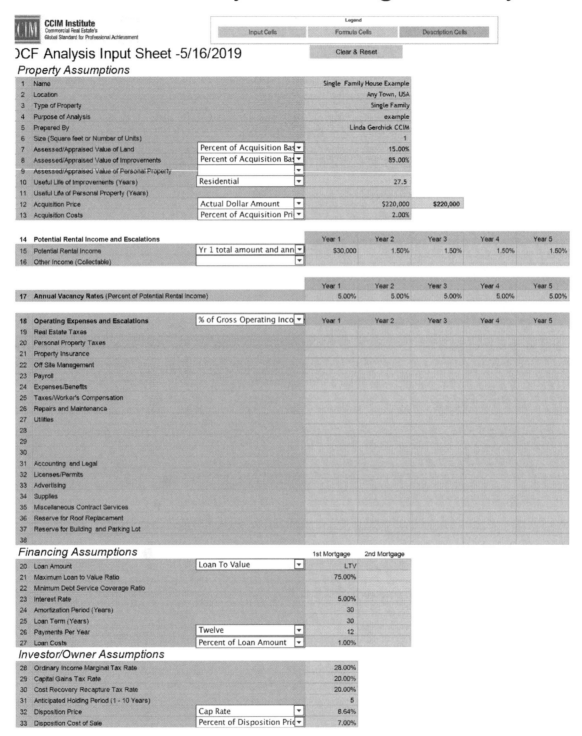

Reprinted with permission of the CCIM Institute / Copyright © 2015

CHAPTER 14 — HOW TO USE AND UNDERSTAND SPREADSHEETS

Investment Analysis — Single-Family

CCIM Institute
Commercial Real Estate's
Global Standard for Professional Achievement

Cash Flow Analysis Worksheet

Property Name	Single Family House Example	Acquisition Price		$220,000
Location	Any Town, USA	Plus Acquisition Costs		$4,400
Type of Property	Single Family	Plus Loan Costs		$1,650
Size of Property (sf/units)	1	Minus Mortgages		$165,000
Purpose of Analysis	example	Equals Initial Investment		$61,050
Prepared by	Linda Gerchick CCIM			
Date Prepared	May 16, 2019			

MORTGAGE DATA			COST RECOVERY DATA		BASIS DATA	
	1st Mortgage	2nd Mortgage		Improvements	Personal Property	
Amount	$165,000		Value	$190,740		Acquisition Price	$220,000
Interest Rate	5.00%		C. R. Method	SL	SL	Acquisition Costs	$4,400
Amortization Period	30		Useful Life	27.5		Total Acquisition Basis	$224,400
Loan Term	30		In Service Date	1-Jan	1-Jan		
Payments/Year	12		Date of Sale	31-Dec	31-Dec		
Periodic Payment	$885.76		12 Months % age	3.636%			
Annual Debt Service	$10,629		11.5 Months % age	3.485%			
Loan Fees/Costs	$1,650						

TAXABLE INCOME

End of Year		1	2	3	4	5	6	7
1	POTENTIAL RENTAL INCOME	$30,000	$30,450	$30,907	$31,370	$31,841	$32,319	
2	-Vacancy & Credit Losses	$1,500	$1,523	$1,545	$1,569	$1,592	$1,616	
3	EFFECTIVE RENTAL INCOME	$28,500	$28,928	$29,361	$29,802	$30,249	$30,703	
4	+Other Income (collectable)							
5	GROSS OPERATING INCOME	$28,500	$28,928	$29,361	$29,802	$30,249	$30,703	
6	TOTAL OPERATING EXPENSES	$8,550	$8,678	$8,808	$8,941	$9,075	$9,211	
7	NET OPERATING INCOME	$19,950	$20,249	$20,553	$20,861	$21,174	$21,492	
8	-Interest-First Mortgage	$8,196	$8,070	$7,938	$7,802	$7,657		
9	-Interest-Second Mortgage							
10	-Cost Recovery-Improvements	$6,647	$6,935	$6,935	$6,935	$6,647		
11	-Cost Recovery-Personal Property							
12	-Loan Costs Amortization	$55	$55	$55	$55	$55		
13	-							
14	-							
15	REAL ESTATE TAXABLE INCOME	$5,052	$5,189	$5,624	$6,070	$6,815		
16	Tax Liability (Savings) at 28.0%	$1,415	$1,453	$1,575	$1,699	$1,908		

CASH FLOW

		1	2	3	4	5	6	7
17	NET OPERATING INCOME (Line 7)	$19,950	$20,249	$20,553	$20,861	$21,174		
18	-Annual Debt Service	$10,629	$10,629	$10,629	$10,629	$10,629		
19	-							
20	-							
21	-							
22	CASH FLOW BEFORE TAXES	$9,321	$9,620	$9,924	$10,232	$10,545		
23	-Tax Liability (Savings) (Line 16)	$1,415	$1,453	$1,575	$1,699	$1,908		
24	CASH FLOW AFTER TAXES	$7,906	$8,167	$8,349	$8,533	$8,637		

Reprinted with permission of the CCIM Institute / Copyright © 2015

LINDA GERCHICK'S PRACTICAL GUIDE TO COMMERCIAL REAL ESTATE

Investment Analysis — Single-Family

CCIM Institute
Commercial Real Estate's
Global Standard for Professional Achievement

Cash Sale Worksheet

MORTGAGE BALANCES

1	End of Year:	1	2	3	4	5
2	Principal Balance - 1st Mortgage	$162,566	$160,008	$157,318	$154,490	$151,518
3	Principal Balance - 2nd Mortgage					
4	TOTAL UNPAID BALANCE	$162,566	$160,008	$157,318	$154,490	$151,518

CALCULATION OF SALE PROCEEDS

5	END OF YEAR	1	2	3	4	5
6	PROJECTED SALES PRICE (Rounded to nearest 000)					$249,000

CALCULATION OF ADJUSTED BASIS

7	Basis at Acquisition					$224,400
8	+Capital Additions					
9	-Cost Recovery (Depreciation) Taken					$34,099
10	-Basis in Partial Sales					
11	=Adjusted Basis at Sale					$190,301

CALCULATION OF CAPITAL GAIN ON SALE

12	Sale Price					$249,000
13	-Costs of Sale					$17,430
14	-Adjusted Basis at Sale (Line 11)					$190,301
15	-					
16	=Gain or (Loss)					$41,269
17	-Straight Line Cost Recovery (limited to gain) (Line 9)					$34,099
18	-Suspended Losses					
19	=Capital Gain from Appreciation					$7,170

ITEMS TAXED AS ORDINARY INCOME

20	Unamortized Loan Fees/Costs (negative)					($1,375)
21	+					
22	=Ordinary Taxable Income					($1,375)

CALCULATION OF SALE PROCEEDS

23	Sale Price					$249,000
24	Cost of Sale					$17,430
25	-Participation Payments on Sale					
26	-Mortgage Balance(s)					$151,518
27	+Balance of Funded Reserves					
28	=SALE PROCEEDS BEFORE TAX					$80,052
29	-Tax (Savings)on Ordinary Income (Line 22 x 28.0%)					($385)
30	-Tax on Cost Recovery Recapture (Line 17 x 20%)					$6,820
31	-Tax on Capital Gain (Line 19 x 20%)					$1,434
32	=SALE PROCEEDS AFTER TAX					$72,183

Reprinted with permission of the CCIM Institute / Copyright © 2015

CHAPTER 14 — HOW TO USE AND UNDERSTAND SPREADSHEETS

Investment Analysis — Single-Family

Measures of Investment Performance

	Before Tax			After Tax	
EOY	$		EOY	$	
IRR =	20.24%		IRR =	16.18%	
NPV @		=	NPV @		=

End of Year	1	2	3	4	5	6
Value Using Acquisition Cap Rate	$223,000	$227,000	$230,000	$233,000	$237,000	
Loan Balance	$162,566	$160,007	$157,317	$154,489	$151,517	
Loan to Value	72.90%	70.49%	68.40%	66.30%	63.93%	
Debt Service Coverage Ratio	1.88	1.91	1.93	1.96	1.99	
Return on Asset	9.07%	9.20%	9.34%	9.48%	9.62%	
Before Tax Cash on Cash	15.27%	15.76%	16.26%	16.76%	17.27%	
After Tax Cash on Cash	12.95%	13.38%	13.68%	13.98%	14.15%	
Acquisition Cap Rate	9.07%					
Gross Rent Multiplier	7.33					
Effective Tax Rate	20.08%					

Proof of Before Tax IRR

EOY	Cash Flows	Sale Proceeds
	($61,050)	
1	$9,321	
2	$9,620	
3	$9,924	
4	$10,232	
5	$10,545	+ $80,052

IRR = 20.24%

Year	Beginning Investment Amount	+	Amount Earned/ Return On	=	Beginning Amount Plus Amount Earned	−	Amount Withdrawn/ Cash Flow	=	Ending Investment Amount	Return Of
1	$61,050	+	$12,359	=	$73,409	−	$9,321	=	$64,088	($3,038)
2	$64,088	+	$12,974	=	$77,061	−	$9,620	=	$67,441	($3,353)
3	$67,441	+	$13,652	=	$81,094	−	$9,924	=	$71,170	($3,729)
4	$71,170	+	$14,407	=	$85,577	−	$10,232	=	$75,345	($4,175)
5	$75,345	+	$15,252	=	$90,597	−	$90,597	=		$75,345
Totals			$68,644				$129,694			$61,050

Reprinted with permission of the CCIM Institute / Copyright © 2015

LINDA GERCHICK'S PRACTICAL GUIDE TO COMMERCIAL REAL ESTATE

Investment Analysis — Fourplex

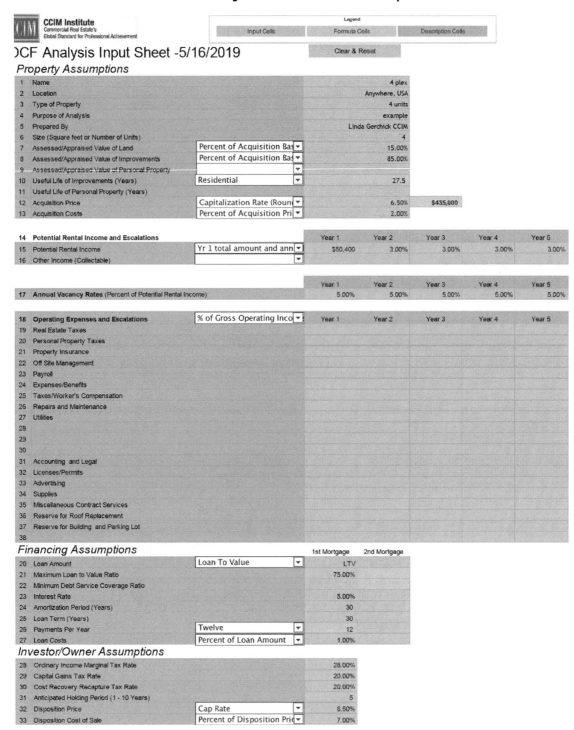

Reprinted with permission of the CCIM Institute / Copyright © 2015

CHAPTER 14 — HOW TO USE AND UNDERSTAND SPREADSHEETS

Investment Analysis — Fourplex

CCIM Institute
Commercial Real Estate's
Global Standard for Professional Achievement

Cash Flow Analysis Worksheet

Property Name	4 plex	Acquisition Price		$435,000
Location	Anywhere, USA	Plus Acquisition Costs		$8,700
Type of Property	4 units	Plus Loan Costs		$3,263
Size of Property (sf/units)	4	Minus Mortgages		$326,250
Purpose of Analysis	example	Equals Initial Investment		$120,713
Prepared by	Linda Gerchick CCIM			
Date Prepared	May 16, 2019			

MORTGAGE DATA			COST RECOVERY DATA			BASIS DATA	
	1st Mortgage	2nd Mortgage		Improvements	Personal Property		
Amount	$326,250		Value	$377,145		Acquisition Price	$435,000
Interest Rate	5.00%		C. R. Method	SL	SL	Acquisition Costs	$8,700
Amortization Period	30		Useful Life	27.5		Total Acquisition Basis	$443,700
Loan Term	30		In Service Date	1-Jan	1-Jan		
Payments/Year	12		Date of Sale	31-Dec	31-Dec		
Periodic Payment	$1,751.38		12 Months % age	3.636%			
Annual Debt Service	$21,017		11.5 Months % age	3.485%			
Loan Fees/Costs	$3,263						

TAXABLE INCOME

	End of Year	1	2	3	4	5	6	7
1	POTENTIAL RENTAL INCOME	$50,400	$51,912	$53,469	$55,073	$56,726	$58,427	
2	-Vacancy & Credit Losses	$2,520	$2,596	$2,673	$2,754	$2,836	$2,921	
3	EFFECTIVE RENTAL INCOME	$47,880	$49,316	$50,796	$52,320	$53,889	$55,506	
4	+Other Income (collectable)							
5	GROSS OPERATING INCOME	$47,880	$49,316	$50,796	$52,320	$53,889	$55,506	
6	TOTAL OPERATING EXPENSES	$19,631	$20,220	$20,826	$21,451	$22,095	$22,757	
7	NET OPERATING INCOME	$28,249	$29,097	$29,970	$30,869	$31,795	$32,749	
8	-Interest-First Mortgage	$16,203	$15,957	$15,698	$15,426	$15,140		
9	-Interest-Second Mortgage							
10	-Cost Recovery-Improvements	$13,144	$13,713	$13,713	$13,713	$13,144		
11	-Cost Recovery-Personal Property							
12	-Loan Costs Amortization	$109	$109	$109	$109	$109		
13	-							
14	-							
15	REAL ESTATE TAXABLE INCOME	($1,207)	($682)	$450	$1,621	$3,402		
16	Tax Liability (Savings) at 28.0%	($338)	($191)	$126	$454	$953		

CASH FLOW

		1	2	3	4	5	6	7
17	NET OPERATING INCOME (Line 7)	$28,249	$29,097	$29,970	$30,869	$31,795		
18	-Annual Debt Service	$21,017	$21,017	$21,017	$21,017	$21,017		
19	-							
20	-							
21	-							
22	CASH FLOW BEFORE TAXES	$7,233	$8,080	$8,953	$9,852	$10,778		
23	-Tax Liability (Savings) (Line 16)	($338)	($191)	$126	$454	$953		
24	CASH FLOW AFTER TAXES	$7,570	$8,271	$8,827	$9,398	$9,826		

Reprinted with permission of the CCIM Institute / Copyright © 2015

LINDA GERCHICK'S PRACTICAL GUIDE TO COMMERCIAL REAL ESTATE

Investment Analysis — Fourplex

Cash Sale Worksheet

MORTGAGE BALANCES

1	End of Year:	1	2	3	4	5
2	Principal Balance - 1st Mortgage	$321,437	$316,377	$311,058	$305,468	$299,591
3	Principal Balance - 2nd Mortgage					
4	TOTAL UNPAID BALANCE	$321,437	$316,377	$311,058	$305,468	$299,591

CALCULATION OF SALE PROCEEDS

5	END OF YEAR	1	2	3	4	5
6	PROJECTED SALES PRICE (Rounded to nearest 000)					$504,000

CALCULATION OF ADJUSTED BASIS

7	Basis at Acquisition					$443,700
8	+Capital Additions					
9	-Cost Recovery (Depreciation) Taken					$67,427
10	-Basis in Partial Sales					
11	=Adjusted Basis at Sale					$376,273

CALCULATION OF CAPITAL GAIN ON SALE

12	Sale Price					$504,000
13	-Costs of Sale					$35,280
14	-Adjusted Basis at Sale (Line 11)					$376,273
15	-					
16	=Gain or (Loss)					$92,447
17	-Straight Line Cost Recovery (limited to gain) (Line 9)					$67,427
18	-Suspended Losses					
19	=Capital Gain from Appreciation					$25,020

ITEMS TAXED AS ORDINARY INCOME

20	Unamortized Loan Fees/Costs (negative)					($2,719)
21	+					
22	=Ordinary Taxable Income					($2,719)

CALCULATION OF SALE PROCEEDS

23	Sale Price					$504,000
24	Cost of Sale					$35,280
25	-Participation Payments on Sale					
26	-Mortgage Balance(s)					$299,591
27	+Balance of Funded Reserves					
28	=SALE PROCEEDS BEFORE TAX					$169,129
29	-Tax (Savings)on Ordinary Income (Line 22 x 28.0%)					($761)
30	-Tax on Cost Recovery Recapture (Line 17 x 20%)					$13,485
31	-Tax on Capital Gain (Line 19 x 20%)					$5,004
32	=SALE PROCEEDS AFTER TAX					$151,401

Reprinted with permission of the CCIM Institute / Copyright © 2015

Investment Analysis — Fourplex

Measures of Investment Performance

	Before Tax			After Tax	
EOY	$		EOY	$	
IRR =	13.40%		IRR =	11.24%	
NPV @		=	NPV @		=

End of Year	1	2	3	4	5	6
Value Using Acquisition Cap Rate	$448,000	$461,000	$475,000	$490,000	$504,000	
Loan Balance	$321,437	$316,377	$311,058	$305,468	$299,591	
Loan to Value	71.75%	68.63%	65.49%	62.34%	59.44%	
Debt Service Coverage Ratio	1.34	1.38	1.43	1.47	1.51	
Return on Asset	6.49%	6.69%	6.89%	7.10%	7.31%	
Before Tax Cash on Cash	5.99%	6.69%	7.42%	8.16%	8.93%	
After Tax Cash on Cash	6.27%	6.85%	7.31%	7.79%	8.14%	
Acquisition Cap Rate	6.49%					
Gross Rent Multiplier	8.63					
Effective Tax Rate	16.13%					

Proof of Before Tax IRR

EOY	Cash Flows	Sale Proceeds							
			IRR = 13.40%						
Year	Beginning Investment Amount	+	Amount Earned/ Return On	=	Beginning Amount Plus Amount Earned	-	Amount Withdrawn/ Cash Flow	=	Ending Investment Amount	Return Of
Totals			$93,312				$214,025			$120,712

Reprinted with permission of the CCIM Institute / Copyright © 2015

Investment Analysis — 10-Unit

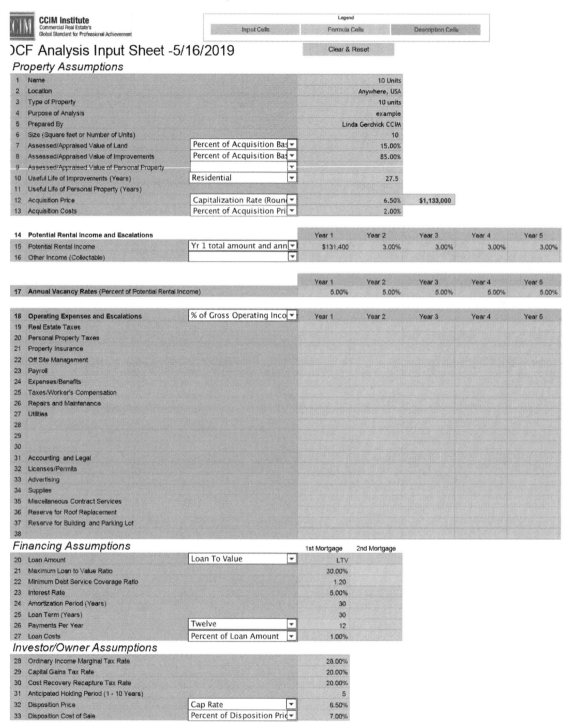

Investment Analysis — 10-Unit

Cash Flow Analysis Worksheet

Property Name	10 Units	Acquisition Price		$1,133,000
Location	Anywhere, USA	Plus Acquisition Costs		$22,660
Type of Property	10 units	Plus Loan Costs		$3,399
Size of Property (sf/units)	10	Minus Mortgages		$339,900
Purpose of Analysis	example	Equals Initial Investment		$819,159
Prepared by	Linda Gerchick CCIM			
Date Prepared	May 16, 2019			

MORTGAGE DATA			COST RECOVERY DATA			BASIS DATA	
	1st Mortgage	2nd Mortgage		Improvements	Personal Property		
Amount	$339,900		Value	$982,311		Acquisition Price	$1,133,000
Interest Rate	5.00%		C. R. Method	SL	SL	Acquisition Costs	$22,660
Amortization Period	30		Useful Life	27.5		Total Acquisition Basis	$1,155,660
Loan Term	30		In Service Date	1-Jan	1-Jan		
Payments/Year	12		Date of Sale	31-Dec	31-Dec		
Periodic Payment	$1,824.66		12 Months % age	3.636%			
Annual Debt Service	$21,896		11.5 Months % age	3.485%			
Loan Fees/Costs	$3,399						

TAXABLE INCOME

End of Year		1	2	3	4	5	6	7
1	POTENTIAL RENTAL INCOME	$131,400	$135,342	$139,402	$143,584	$147,892	$152,329	
2	-Vacancy & Credit Losses	$6,570	$6,767	$6,970	$7,179	$7,395	$7,616	
3	EFFECTIVE RENTAL INCOME	$124,830	$128,575	$132,432	$136,405	$140,497	$144,712	
4	+Other Income (collectable)							
5	GROSS OPERATING INCOME	$124,830	$128,575	$132,432	$136,405	$140,497	$144,712	
6	TOTAL OPERATING EXPENSES	$51,180	$52,716	$54,297	$55,926	$57,604	$59,332	
7	NET OPERATING INCOME	$73,650	$75,859	$78,135	$80,479	$82,893	$85,380	
8	-Interest-First Mortgage	$16,882	$16,625	$16,355	$16,071	$15,773		
9	-Interest-Second Mortgage							
10	-Cost Recovery-Improvements	$34,234	$35,717	$35,717	$35,717	$34,234		
11	-Cost Recovery-Personal Property							
12	-Loan Costs Amortization	$113	$113	$113	$113	$113		
13	-							
14	-							
15	REAL ESTATE TAXABLE INCOME	$22,421	$23,404	$25,950	$28,577	$32,773		
16	Tax Liability (Savings) at 28.0%	$6,278	$6,553	$7,266	$8,002	$9,176		

CASH FLOW

		1	2	3	4	5	6	7
17	NET OPERATING INCOME (Line 7)	$73,650	$75,859	$78,135	$80,479	$82,893		
18	-Annual Debt Service	$21,896	$21,896	$21,896	$21,896	$21,896		
19	-							
20	-							
21	-							
22	CASH FLOW BEFORE TAXES	$51,754	$53,963	$56,239	$58,583	$60,997		
23	-Tax Liability (Savings) (Line 16)	$6,278	$6,553	$7,266	$8,002	$9,176		
24	CASH FLOW AFTER TAXES	$45,476	$47,410	$48,973	$50,581	$51,821		

Reprinted with permission of the CCIM Institute / Copyright © 2015

Investment Analysis — 10-Unit

Cash Sale Worksheet

MORTGAGE BALANCES

1	End of Year:	1	2	3	4	5
2	Principal Balance - 1st Mortgage	$334,886	$329,615	$324,073	$318,249	$312,126
3	Principal Balance - 2nd Mortgage					
4	TOTAL UNPAID BALANCE	$334,886	$329,615	$324,073	$318,249	$312,126

CALCULATION OF SALE PROCEEDS

5	END OF YEAR	1	2	3	4	5
6	PROJECTED SALES PRICE (Rounded to nearest 000)					$1,314,000

CALCULATION OF ADJUSTED BASIS

7	Basis at Acquisition					$1,155,660
8	+Capital Additions					
9	-Cost Recovery (Depreciation) Taken					$175,619
10	-Basis in Partial Sales					
11	=Adjusted Basis at Sale					$980,041

CALCULATION OF CAPITAL GAIN ON SALE

12	Sale Price					$1,314,000
13	-Costs of Sale					$91,980
14	-Adjusted Basis at Sale (Line 11)					$980,041
15	-					
16	=Gain or (Loss)					$241,979
17	-Straight Line Cost Recovery (limited to gain) (Line 9)					$175,619
18	-Suspended Losses					
19	=Capital Gain from Appreciation					$66,360

ITEMS TAXED AS ORDINARY INCOME

20	Unamortized Loan Fees/Costs (negative)					($2,833)
21	+					
22	=Ordinary Taxable Income					($2,833)

CALCULATION OF SALE PROCEEDS

23	Sale Price					$1,314,000
24	Cost of Sale					$91,980
25	-Participation Payments on Sale					
26	-Mortgage Balance(s)					$312,126
27	+Balance of Funded Reserves					
28	=SALE PROCEEDS BEFORE TAX					$909,894
29	-Tax (Savings)on Ordinary Income (Line 22 x 28.0%)					($793)
30	-Tax on Cost Recovery Recapture (Line 17 x 20%)					$35,124
31	-Tax on Capital Gain (Line 19 x 20%)					$13,272
32	=SALE PROCEEDS AFTER TAX					$862,291

Reprinted with permission of the CCIM Institute / Copyright © 2015

CHAPTER 14 — HOW TO USE AND UNDERSTAND SPREADSHEETS

Investment Analysis — 10-Unit

Measures of Investment Performance

	Before Tax			After Tax	
EOY	$		EOY	$	
IRR =	8.69%		IRR =	6.86%	
NPV @		=	NPV @		=

End of Year	1	2	3	4	5	6
Value Using Acquisition Cap Rate	$1,167,000	$1,202,000	$1,238,000	$1,275,000	$1,313,000	
Loan Balance	$334,885	$329,614	$324,073	$318,248	$312,126	
Loan to Value	28.70%	27.42%	26.18%	24.96%	23.77%	
Debt Service Coverage Ratio	3.36	3.46	3.57	3.68	3.79	
Return on Asset	6.50%	6.70%	6.90%	7.10%	7.32%	
Before Tax Cash on Cash	6.32%	6.59%	6.87%	7.15%	7.45%	
After Tax Cash on Cash	5.55%	5.79%	5.98%	6.17%	6.33%	
Acquisition Cap Rate	6.50%					
Gross Rent Multiplier	8.62					
Effective Tax Rate	21.10%					

Proof of Before Tax IRR

EOY	Cash Flows	Sale Proceeds				
		IRR = 8.69%				
Year	Beginning Investment Amount	+ Amount Earned/ Return On	= Beginning Amount Plus Amount Earned	- Amount Withdrawn/ Cash Flow	= Ending Investment Amount	Return Of
Totals		$372,271		$1,191,430		$819,159

Reprinted with permission of the CCIM Institute / Copyright © 2015

INVESTING GLOSSARY

A

Accumulated cost recovery — Total cost recovery deductions taken throughout the holding period of a property.

Active income — Income from salary, wages, tips, commissions and other activities in which the taxpayer participates.

Adjusted basis — The original cost basis of a property plus capital improvements, less total accumulated cost recovery deductions and partial sales taken during the holding period.

Amortization — The repayment of loan principal through equal payments over a designated period of time.

Annual debt service (ADS) — The total amount of principal and interest to be paid each year to satisfy the obligations of a loan contract.

Annuity — Regular fixed payments or receipts over a designated period of time.

Appreciation — An investment's increase in value.

Appreciation potential — The possibility or probability that a real estate investment will increase in value during the holding period.

Assessed value — The value of real property established by the tax assessor for the purpose of levying real estate taxes.

B

Balloon payment — The final payment of the balance due on a partially amortized loan.

Base rent — The minimum monthly rent due to the landlord (typically, a fixed amount).

Basis — The total amount paid for a property, including equity capital and the amount of debt incurred.

Before-tax investment value — The sum of the present values of the mortgagor and mortgagee of property.

Business risk — The uncertainty associated with the possible profit outcomes of a business venture.

C

Capital gain — Taxable income derived from the sale of a capital asset. It is equal to the sale price less the cost of sale; adjusted basis, suspended losses, excess cost recovery and recapture of straight-line recovery.

Capitalization — The process of converting the future net operating income of an income-producing property into a single present value, given a capitalization rate.

Capitalization rate — A percentage that relates the value of an income-producing property to its future income, expressed as net operating income divided by price.

Cash flow after taxes (CFAT) — The periodic amounts of money received by an investor after taxes from the operations of a real estate investment.

Cash flow before taxes (CFBT) — The periodic amounts of money received by an investor after taxes from the operations of a real estate investment.

Cash flow model — The framework used to determine the cash flow from operations and the cash proceeds from sale.

Cash flows — Investment returns generated by one of two methods: current income (rents, dividends, etc.) minus expenses and debt service or cash proceeds received upon the sale of an investment (reversion).

Cash-on-cash rate — A simple return measure. Calculated as cash flow before taxes divided by initial equity investment.

Cash proceeds from sale — The sale proceeds less sale costs, mortgage balance, and tax liability on sale. Also called the "sale proceed after taxes."

Class life — The useful economic life of an asset set by the IRS.

Compound interest — Interest computed on the original principal and accumulated interest.

Compounding — A type of calculation in which the interest earned is reinvested and earns additional interest.

Cost — The actual dollar amount paid for a property or the amount needed to build or improve it at a specified time in the future.

Cost approach — A way to determine the market value of the property by evaluating the costs of creating a property exactly like the subject.

Cost recovery — An annual deduction based on the class life of an asset.

D

Debt coverage ratio (DCR) — Ratio of net operating income to annual debt service. Expressed as NOI divided by ADS.

Depreciation — The loss of utility and value of a property.

Discounting — The process of reducing the value of money received in the future to reflect the opportunity cost of waiting to receive the money.

Diversification — A method of reducing risk by investing in unrelated (uncorrelated) assets.

E

Economic obsolescence — The reduction in a property's value due to external circumstances such as legislation or changes in nearby property use.

Equilibrium point — The price at which the quantity supplied equals the quantity demanded.

Equity yield rate — The return on the portion of an investment financed by equity capital.

F

Financial leverage — The use of borrowed funds to acquire an investment.

Financial risk — The possible change in an investment's ability to return principal and income.

Fixed expenses — Costs that do not change with a building's occupancy rate. They include property taxes, insurance and some forms of building maintenance.

Fully amortized mortgage loan — A method of loan amortization in which equal periodic payments fully repay the loan.

Functional obsolescence — The reduced capacity of a property or improvements to perform their intended functions due to new technology, poor design or changes in the market standard.

Future value — The amount to which money grows over a designated period of time at a specified rate of interest.

G

Gross operating income — The total amount of cash generated by the operations of a property.

H

Hedging — Protecting oneself against negative outcomes.

I

I — A component of the T-Bar which represents the interest rate.

Imperfect market — A market in which product differentiation exists, there is a lack of important product information, and certain buyers or sellers may influence the market. Commercial real estate is bought and sold in an imperfect market.

Income capitalization approach — A way to determine the market value of an income-producing property by converting its future income stream into a single capital value.

Initial investment — The outlay of cash needed to acquire an investment.

Insurable value — The value of the portions of the property that are physically destructible.

Interest rate — The lender's rate of return on borrowed money.

Interest-only loan — A method of loan amortization in which interest is paid periodically over the term of the loan and the entire loan amount is paid at maturity.

Internal rate of return (IRR) — The percentage rate earned on each dollar that remains in an investment each year. The IRR of an investment is the discount rate at which the sum of the present value of future cash flows equals the initial capital investment.

Investing — Limiting current consumption in favor of future consumption.

Investment value — The value to a specific investor, based on that investor's requirements, tax rate, financing, etc.

L

Lease — A contract between landlords and tenants for a possession of space for a specified amount of rent. Leases are used for all types of properties.

Leverage — The use of borrowed funds to finance a portion of the cost of an investment.

Liquidation value — The likely price that a property would bring in a forced sale (foreclosure or tax sale). Used when a sale must occur with limited exposure time to market or with restrictive conditions of sale.

Liquidity — The ability to convert an investment into cash quickly without loss of principal.

Loan balance — The amount of money remaining to be paid on an amortizing loan at a given time.

Loan or mortgage value — That portion of the value of real property recognized by the lender when used to secure a loan.

Loan point — A charge prepaid by the borrower upon the origination of a loan. On point equals one percent of the loan amount.

Loan-to-value (LTV) ratio — The amount of money borrowed in relation to the total market value of a property. Expressed as the loan amount divided by the property value.

M

Management — The ability to monitor the performance of an investment and make changes as needed.

Market risk — The possibility that downward market trends will reduce an investment's market value.

Managing risk — The steps taken by an investor to mitigate risk.

Market value — The most probable price that a property would bring in a competitive and open market under "fair sale" conditions. Market value also refers to an estimate of this price.

Market — The process of exchange, where one person or group can exchange one kind of product with another person or group.

Marketability — The ability to sell an investment quickly regardless of its sales price.

N

N — A component of the T-Bar that represents the number of periods over which the investment is held.

Negative leverage — Borrowed funds are invested at a rate of return lower than the cost of funds to the borrower.

Net operating income (NOI) — The potential rental income plus other income, less vacancy, credit losses, and operating expenses.

Neutral expenses — An investment situation where the cost of borrowed funds is exactly equal to the yield provided by the investment.

O

Operating expenses — Cash outlays necessary to operate and maintain a property.

Opportunity cost — The "cost" of selecting one alternative is the benefit foregone from the next best alternative.

Original basis — The total amount paid for a property, including equity capital and the amount of debt incurred.

P

Partially amortized mortgage loan — The payments do not repay the loan over its term and thus a lump sum (balloon) is required to repay the loan.

Passive income — Income from rental activity, limited business interests, or other activities in which the investor does not materially participate.

Passive losses — Losses from the ownership of passive investments.

Payment — A periodic amount paid or received for two or more periods.

Perfect market — A market in which the products are homogenous, there is complete information, and no buyers or sellers may influence the market.

Periodic cash flow — The amount of income received periodically (rents, dividends, etc.)

Perpetuity — A form of annuity in which an amount is received at the end of the period (a year, a month) forever.

Physical depreciation — The physical decay or deterioration of a property.

Portfolio income — Income from interest, dividends, royalties, or the disposition of property held for an investment.

Positive leverage — Borrowed funds are invested at a rate of return higher that the cost of the funds to the borrower.

Potential rental income — The total amount of rental income for a property if it were 100% occupied and rented at competitive market rates.

Present value — The sum of all future benefits accruing to the owner of an asset when such benefits are discounted to the present by an appropriate discount rate.

Price — The dollar amount that was offered, asked, or actually paid for a property.

Principal — The portion of the loan payment used toward reducing the original loan amount.

Property type — The classification of commercial investment real estate. The four primary property types are: retail, industrial, office and residential.

Purchasing power risk — The variability in the future purchasing power of income received from an investment.

R

Rate of return — The percentage return on each dollar invested. Also known as yield.

Recapture — Taxable income derived from the sale of a capital asset. It is equal to the amount of straight-line cost recovery taken during the holding period.

Reversion — The cash received upon the sale of an investment.

Risk — The probability that actual cash flows from an investment will vary from the forecasted cash flows.

S

Safe rate — The rate a low-risk, liquid investment achieves.

Sales comparison approach — A way to determine market value by comparing a subject property to properties with the same or similar characteristics.

Sales proceeds before tax—The sale price minus the sale costs and the mortgage loan balance.

Sale cost — The brokerage commission and fees, and any additional transaction costs that are incurred during the sale of the property.

Sale price — The total amount paid to the seller at time of sale.

Sale proceeds after tax — The sale proceeds before tax minus the liability on the sale.

Sinking fund — A fund designed to accumulate a designated amount of money over a specified period of time. The periodic amount of money deposited plus compound interest will accumulate to the designated amount of money over the specified period of time.

Sunk costs — Investment costs that are committed and cannot be recovered.

Supply — The amount of property that will be made available for sale or rent at a given price or rental rate.

Suspended losses — Passive losses that cannot be used in the current year are "suspended" for use in future years or at the time of sale.

T

T-Bar — A chart used to summarize the timing of real estate cash flows.

Tax impact — The impact of taxes on investment income and rate of return.

Tax liability — Real estate taxable income multiplied by the tax rate.

Tax shelter — The ability of real estate holdings to reduce an investor's tax liability through the use of cost recovery.

Taxable income — Adjusted gross income less personal deductions and exemptions.

Taxation — How an investment is affected by tax laws and codes.

Time value of money (TVM) — An economic principle recognizing that a dollar today has greater value in the future because of its earning power.

V

Variable expenses — Costs, such as utilities, that vary with a building's occupancy rate.

Y

Yield — A measure of investment performance, gauging the percentage return on each dollar invested. Also known as rate of return.

CONTACT INFORMATION

Linda Gerchick, CCIM

Linda@JustSoldIt.com

602-688-9279
4602 E. Waltann Lane
Phoenix, AZ 85032
www.JustSoldIt.com

Made in the USA
Columbia, SC
30 April 2025

57338564R00079